My Brooklyn, My Way

My Brooklyn, My Way

From Brownsville to Canarsie in the 1950's

MARTIN LEWIS BLUMBERG

Copyright © 2020 by Martin Lewis Blumberg.

Library of Congress Control Number:		2019918171
ISBN:	Hardcover	978-1-7960-7067-5
	Softcover	978-1-7960-7066-8
	eBook	978-1-7960-7065-1

All rights reserved. No part of this book may be reproduced or transmitted in any form or by any means, electronic or mechanical, including photocopying, recording, or by any information storage and retrieval system, without permission in writing from the copyright owner.

The views expressed in this work are solely those of the author and do not necessarily reflect the views of the publisher, and the publisher hereby disclaims any responsibility for them.

Any people depicted in stock imagery provided by Getty Images are models, and such images are being used for illustrative purposes only.
Certain stock imagery © Getty Images.

Print information available on the last page.

Rev. date: 01/15/2020

To order additional copies of this book, contact:
Xlibris
1-888-795-4274
www.Xlibris.com
Orders@Xlibris.com
798856

Contents

Foreword ix
Acknowledgments xiii
Introduction xv

History of Brooklyn 1
Born in Brooklyn 4
Our Telephone 8
The Public Phone 9
Family Planning 11
Sleeping 13
The Blumberg Boys 15
Amboy Street 17
My Mother 20
Cooking 22
My Father 24
Bob 27
Annie Hunk 29
Herb 33
Jack 36
Bruce 38
Batboy for a Day 40
Trek to Canarsie 42
Grocery Shopping 44
Icebox 45
Betsy Head Pool 46
Chinatown 49
Catskills 51
Tradition 54
Amboy Street was starting to get Shabby 55
Larry Aaron 57
Red Goldstein and his brother Heshy 58

Things I Remember 60
Things we did as Kids that could have gotten us Killed 64
Lundy's 67
Coney Island Joe's 69
Family Business 70
The Spaldeen and Stoopball 72
Stores in the Area 74
Holidays 76
School 78
The Lone Ranger 83
Horn & Hardart 84
Music 85
S&H Stamps or was it King Korn Stamps? 87
Family Values 88
There was always a Blumberg 89
Toys 90
Shoemaker 91
Movies 93
Choir 95
Hebrew School 97
Barbershop 98
First TV Set 100
These Were Some of the Games I Played in the Streets 103
Games Girls Played 105
Baseball 106
Topps 108
Moshe at the Bat (Poem) 109
Baseball 113
I Remember Stickball 115
Brooklyn Dodgers 117
Post Office (Poem) 119
Canarsie History 121
Getting Ready for Canarsie 122
Canarsie, My New Home 124
Lloyd 60 126
Coney Island 129
I Ran All the Way Home 132
People from Bayview 134

Mike Tyson from Amboy Street 136
My Philosophy of Memories 138
We Met at a Dance 140
The Remote 143
I Do the Shopping 145
Taking a Swing at Golf 147
Grabstein's Kosher Delicatessen 149
Comments from Friends 151
Thomas Jefferson High School 158
Non Graduates from Brooklyn 161
Life goes by Fast (Poem) 162
Going Back To Brownsville (Poem) 164
My Brooklyn, My Way (Poem) 165

Epilogue 181
Index 183

Foreword

Growing up in Brownsville was special, but "special" begs for a definition. Of course, growing up anywhere at any time is special. Special could most likely be substituted for "different." But every time is different, and so is every place. And surely, Brownsville was different in so many ways from any other place or time. What made Brownsville so different back then is that growing up there was filtered through our fresh eyes and ears and, of course, our own interactions with the people we grew up with and the buildings, institutions, and merchants we encountered.

Brownsville in the 1940s up through the early 1960s was a dirty, dingy, and gritty place. But didn't really notice it much because we had nothing to compare it with. It's not that there weren't "better" places to compare it with. We just lived our lives back then in the confines of a few surrounding blocks, never venturing much farther away to explore. That would come later.

While growing up in Brownsville, most of the buildings had been around since the turn of the century when the Brooklyn Bridge provided the means for expansion eastward out of the overcrowded Lower Manhattan toward Long Island. But at the turn of the century, the Brownsville section of Brooklyn was rapidly changing from farmland (Mr. Brown's farm) to the home of the new immigrant families exiting Lower Manhattan. The new IRT subway line even had a stop called New Lots Avenue, where new lots were available for home building. The elevated trains led the way to the expanded areas of new home development.

And then time and circumstance took its toll. The Rockaway Avenue trolley came to an end. Buildings aged further as the "war babies" grew up. In a blink of an eye, properties were becoming over fifty years old, and banks stopped lending to building owners if there were "blacks" living on the block. The shameful era of "redlining" was taking its toll. The only thing left to do was sell those dilapidated and aging buildings to newly arriving Puerto Ricans and blacks who could barely afford them and who found themselves with properties they surely couldn't afford to maintain. It wasn't long before the entire neighborhood was up in flames and ready for complete demolition, razing entire blocks to rubble on the ground.

The new one- and two-family homes that eventually replaced our old neighborhood tenements looked nothing like what once existed there. These new buildings were different, and the new residents were different too, many from the Caribbean islands. The new merchants were different too, and in fact, mostly everything was different. Most of the people who moved out of Brownsville turned their backs on the old neighborhood and, for the most part, were afraid to ever return because the neighborhood became "dangerous." Canarsie was "new" and inviting, so was Staten Island, and the newly built Verrazano Bridge became the exodus roadway from Brooklyn.

So while the new Brownsville was emerging from the ashes of the old, here and there exist vestiges of building facades that survived the changes. The Wu-Han Chinese Restaurant sign on Pitkin Avenue near Saratoga Avenue still hangs with no Chinese restaurant in sight, probably because the sign is too expensive to take down.

Prominent among the old vestiges is the East New York Savings Bank on Pitkin Avenue, now owned by BPPR Popular, and the Lowe's Pitkin movie theater, long under renovation, is now a Dollar Tree. The old Hebrew Educational Society building (HES), our cherished home away from home, became a church and is now under severe renovation with its surrounding scaffolding hiding the work in progress.

The Hebrew Ladies Day Nursery building on Hopkinson Avenue (now Thomas S. Boyland Street) has become the Bethany Gospel Chapel, and the synagogue on Amboy Street around the corner near Sutter Avenue has become Saint Timothy Cathedral. The Hebrew writing still exists on the facade, a strange decoration for a Baptist church. And most interesting is the disappearance of all the old movie theaters. I don't believe a single movie theater exists where before, we had perhaps more than a dozen.

One of the saddest cuts to our Brownsville soul is the street name changes. Stone Avenue has become Mother Gaston Boulevard, and previously mentioned Hopkinson Avenue became Thomas S. Boyland Street, downgraded from an "avenue." And now it appears that even Thomas Jefferson High School has closed its doors, and PS 175 has become a Teachers Preparatory School. Most surprising is the fact that Betsy Head

Pool and its adjacent park are still there and in operation, anchoring our thoughts to a place of fading memories.

Most four-story tenement buildings are gone. All the stores along the shopping street of Sutter Avenue are gone, and no new stores opened to take their place. Stores, it seems, simply aren't needed. People can now get into cars and drive to shopping, whereas back in the day, cars were less ubiquitous, and shopping was done locally and, of course, on foot. How else can you explain why there used to be a drugstore (pharmacy) on every street corner and now there are none, how every block had a candy store or a luncheonette or a barbershop, how there was a delicatessen on every block or every other one? All gone! Since people now use cars for shopping and transportation, almost all the new homes now have driveways and parking spaces for cars, something those four-story tenements utterly lacked.

But Brownsville was changing under our very noses while we lived there. The "projects" (low-income city housing) went up, and many of us hardly even noticed. Most people stayed away from there because of the "low-class element." The all-boys Lew Wallace Junior High School, JHS 66, closed its doors in 1956 and reopened in a brand-new building, becoming Col. David Marcus JHS 263 in that same year. The all-girls junior high, JHS 84 (Glenmore), also merged into JHS 263, and throughout our first year in that new building, it reeked of the delicious scent of freshly curing concrete. It is fascinating to note that many of the teachers in that new building went on to become principals and school superintendents all under the tutelage of Mr. Adolph Dembo, our beloved science teacher and HES counselor.

Brownsville, it should be noted, had the distinct honor of being Margaret Sangar's first birth control and family planning storefront clinic at 46 Amboy Street near the corner of Pitkin Avenue. While she was opposed to abortion, she strongly favored the dissemination of birth control information, which was against the Comstock Law governing "obscenity" at the time. It's interesting to note that most people who grew up in Brownsville who are alive today never even knew of that history. And today, there is not a single plaque on the wall where that storefront existed. Only graffiti-covered, bricked-up windows and doorways mark that historic location.

And finally, a few interesting notes: any old Brownsville resident who chances to walk down Pitkin Avenue as I did a few years ago must come away with the impression that the street appears so much narrower.

The only way I can reconcile that impression is by believing that is what happens when our young brains hold childhood impressions we gathered when everything looked so much bigger because of our smaller statures. Another impression I now come away with is that the storefront signs along the whole avenue just seemed so much "cheaper" and less elegant than they used to be, perhaps reflecting the new lifestyle and economy of the area.

Brownsville, in our day, was truly a magical place as we were growing up, and its image has mellowed over the years in our reveries. Marty Blumberg and I grew up there and proudly share our nostalgic upbringing with you, our dear readers, in the fond hope we can communicate our reverence for a place that no longer exists as we knew it but contributed so much to who we are today.

Roger Elowitz, formerly of 106 Amboy Street, Brooklyn 12, NY

Acknowledgments

This book is dedicated to my wonderful and beautiful wife, Maxine. On March 14, 2019, we celebrated fifty-five years of marriage. I always wanted to write about my memories growing up in Brooklyn, and because of her encouragement, she made my dream come true.

I would also like to thank our three children—Stacey, Richard, and Felicia—for their support and love; without any doubt, they are the best children any parent could wish for. Also, I can't forget their spouses—Noah, Felice, and Jeff—for being a strong part of our family. Thanks to our ten adorable and wonderful grandchildren—Zoe, Jaden, Eliza, Samantha, Jolie, Nate, Max, Miriam, Connor, and Brody—for sharing each great step in life as we watch them grow and accomplish so much. Without my whole family's support and suggestions, this book would never come to fruition. I would also like to thank all you Brooklynites who grew up with me and shared my childhood journey from my childhood days until the present. Also, I can't forget my four brothers whom I shared my experiences and who were always ready and eager to reminisce and discuss all our memories growing up in Brooklyn. This book would not be the same without their thoughts. I always enjoyed the sounds of Frank Sinatra; I feel his inspiration empowered me to live in "My Brooklyn, My Way."

Introduction

I just hope that future generations will read my memoirs and realize how life was in the '50s and that it's not material things that make someone happy but family and friends. I hope these memoirs will teach not only my grandchildren and their children but also kids throughout the world to see what happiness and joy could really be without having or wanting material things.

Being brought up during this era has left memories that are real and unforgettable. When I go to sleep at night, I think about my boyhood years. It relaxes me and gives me a chance to realize how lucky and thankful I am. I am able to visualize and communicate with people I knew growing up in the streets of Brooklyn. I remember their faces and their mannerisms. I realize how much love I had for my mom and dad. In my dreams, I am able to envision that Spaldeen that I misplayed, watching it roll under my legs. I never forget to thank God and express my gratitude for the wonderful life that he has bestowed on me and my family.

History of Brooklyn

When the Dutch settled in Brooklyn in the early seventeenth century, Brooklyn was called Breukelen, named after a small town in Holland. Today, it is the most populated borough in NYC. Brooklyn is also known as Kings County. It's hard to believe that Brooklyn and Queens are part of Long Island. But today, Long Island refers to Nassau and Suffolk County.

At present, over one-third of Brooklynites are foreign born. Up until the nineteenth century, Brooklyn was its own separate city, later merging with the city of New York. Most Brooklynites were against that move and referred to it as the big mistake. But Brooklyn is like no other city in the world, and many popular scholars were born and raised and have enhanced the world we live in today.

Brownsville is less than two square miles in area. Today, it has a reputation of being "Brooklyn's most dangerous neighborhood." Crime rates reached record lows in the borough in 2009, but violence has continued to increase and has remained untouched by gentrification.

But it wasn't always that way. During my boyhood years, Brownsville was considered a safe neighborhood. But since the '50s, most of the infrastructures started to decay and worsen each year.

During the war years of the '40s, thousands of Brownsville residents served in the military. My uncle who was my mother's younger brother, Uncle Izzy, was killed in the Battle of the Bulge. Because he had very poor vision, the Selective Service would have classified him as 4F and unfit for military service. Wanting to serve his country, he enlisted and received the Purple Heart medal.

After World War II ended, the second generation of Jewish people started to immigrate to Brownsville. They were the working-class people who earned a living as peddlers or garment center workers or took jobs wherever they could find work. Since my father was a postman, we were fortunate; he always had a steady job.

In the '50s, Brownsville was recognized as a Jewish community. Pitkin Avenue and Belmont Avenue were the hub of the Jewish community. Synagogues, candy stores, and kosher groceries were prevalent. Most Jewish families did not adhere to orthodox tradition, but there were certain traditions that were followed. We wouldn't ride in a car during the high holidays, and we fasted on Yom Kippur. During the high holidays, we would get dressed with our nicest clothes and walk around the corner a few times. We would make sure we passed the Shul and would hang out with our friends in front of the temple.

About 80 percent of the families living on Amboy Street were Jewish. The other 20 percent were different nationalities that mixed in. I had a few non-Jewish friends but mostly from school. One really close friend that I hung out with was a Polish boy from Amboy Street named Eugene Peotrolski.

By the '60s, Brownsville became very bad. Unemployment, crime, and drug abuse were plentiful, and it was unsafe even to walk out of your building. White people were moving out at a very fast rate, while blacks and Latinos were replacing them. Amboy Street became unrecognizable, along with other streets in Brownsville. Buildings were constantly being burned down, many demolished, and only a few buildings were still standing. The city took over most of these lots. The area was transforming into a very dangerous place. The white population was now a very small percentage.

The government started to build projects to give the people a chance to have better housing. But even that didn't work because the government neglected its development, and Brownsville was getting disastrous.

Hopefully, things will change, and Brownsville can become a vibrant center like it once was with help from politicians and stronger government programs that enhance the business community that would help build and support future developments. They have to stimulate the economy by creating new jobs and pay decent salaries. That alone would increase the standard of living. Also, with the help from institutions, Brownsville can once again prosper. When you examine other areas like Williamsburg,

Red Hook, and Bushwick and see their progress in the last few years, one could see how their landscapes have changed. I believe that the Brownsville community could also change and be rebuilt into a thriving neighborhood like I remember it.

Born in Brooklyn

I was born in Brownsville, Brooklyn in 1941 in a hospital called Beth-El, which in later years had a name change to Brookdale Hospital. It was located on Linden Boulevard at the corner of Rockaway Avenue. The hospital still exists today and has expanded over the years and has served a vital role in the Brooklyn community.

When I was about six months old, we moved from 574 Hopkinson Avenue to 260 Amboy Street, which was a small tenement building consisting of six apartments. Our new apartment had two bedrooms and was on the first floor, facing the street. We seldom locked our door, and there were many times my brothers or I would climb in and out of the window, not because the door was locked but because we didn't want to wake my mom or dad from their sleep. Living on the first floor was an advantage; we never got locked out. The disadvantage was the smell and soot from the coal deliveries that were done outside our front window, and the view of the garbage cans with piled-up garbage was not a very healthy environment. When there was a coal delivery, it would slide down the chute, leaving a cloud of dark ash that would penetrate into our front windows, which made it even more difficult for my mom to take a breath of fresh air. The coal was delivered under our front window into the cellar right where my mom sat every day.

Our rent was twenty-eight dollars a month, a bargain compared with the thirty-three dollars we were paying on Hopkinson Avenue. But that was not the reason we moved. I was told by my three older brothers, and I haven't any memories because I was only an infant, that our apartment on Hopkinson Avenue was so small and crowded that we had no room for a crib. We had a dresser my mom called a chest of drawers. It stored most

My Brooklyn, My Way

of our clothes and took up a whole wall. For the first six months of my life living on Hopkinson Avenue, I slept in this dresser. I started out in the sock drawer, and as I got bigger, I kept on being moved to a larger drawer. By the time we moved to Amboy Street, I was six months old and slept in the large bottom drawer, where we kept our winter sweaters. I think my parents realized we were running out of space, and that was the main reason it was time to move.

During the Christmas holidays, my brothers would hang their socks on this dresser to get them filled with candies. A little unusual for a Jewish family, but I guess it was that time of year when my dad received his Christmas gifts, and since my parents had a little extra money, they wanted to reward their boys. But it did serve another purpose. When I went to sleep in the bottom drawer and looked up, I saw colorful socks hanging above my head. The problem was my brother Jack had a big hole in his sock, and candies would drop into my makeshift bed. Jack's sock was empty by Christmas morning, but he found all the candies in my bed drawer.

Everyone would always say I was the best child. I never complained, very rarely cried, and always seemed content. When we moved to Amboy Street, I moved out of the dresser and into a a crib. It gave me more room to stretch out, and I didn't have to worry about socks above my head or candies falling in my crib.

Our entrance door led into the kitchen. There was a bedroom straight ahead. If you walked to the left, there was our living room, which consisted of a sofa couch that opened into a bed. We had a floor lamp and a bookcase that my father made himself that was filled with books. We had our record player and TV at the foot of the sofa. There was a chair by the window where my mother would greet people walking by and would lean on her pillow called the "rock." You needed two people to lift it because it was filled with feathers from four pillows all made into one. The second bedroom having two beds was to the right of the living room.

Before you entered our bathroom, there was a small pantry where we kept the dishes we got free from the movie theater.

In the center of the cabinet was a drawer that we called our cockamamie drawer. Anything that did not have a place would end up in that drawer. I was in and out that drawer many times because that's where I kept my Spaldeen. It was a place where we kept tools, paperclips, rubber bands, shoelaces, playing cards, my uncle Izzy's trumpet mouthpiece, and even the dice I collected from the broken-up crap games.

The bathroom was to the right of our entranceway from the kitchen. It was very small and just wide enough for one person to enter at a time. Two people could not pass by each other at the same time. One person had to leave before the other could enter. I remember there were many times I had to wait in line behind my brothers to use the bathroom. We did not say anything if one brother had to cut the line being in an urgent situation. Since the bathroom didn't have a sink, we used the kitchen sink to wash and brush our teeth. If there were dishes in the sink, we would move them to the side so the dirty dishes would not get dirtier. This was how life was on Amboy Street, but no one in my family ever complained. We knew this was our way of life, and we were always thankful and happy to have a roof above our heads.

The three-story building we lived in was starting to decay since it was built in the late 1800s. There were two families on each floor. On the top floor lived the husband-and-wife landlords, Minny and Al Krasners. Also on the third (top?) floor was the Sass family, who seemed very old and ill. I always wondered how they were able to walk up three flights of steps each day. On the second floor were the Beckermans and the Cramers. On the first floor at the end of the hallway lived the Schwied family. We had the front apartment overlooking Amboy Street.

We had a backyard alleyway where my mom and neighbors hung their clothes to dry. The clothes would be scrubbed on a washing board and then hung up on a clothesline using clothespins. If an unexpected rain came, it would take another week for the clothes to dry. If you looked out the back window, you could see neighbors talking to one another. Every now and then, you would hear a fiddle or trumpet from men playing their instruments, waiting for a generous tenant to put some change in a napkin and toss it out the window.

I recall a story about our back neighbor Francis Schwied who had two children. The boy's name was Neil and his younger sister's name was Karen. It was unusual at that time, but Mrs. Schwied was divorced. In those days, it was not common for a couple to get a divorce. A day did not go by where Francis would visit my mom to tell about her problems. My mom was a great listener and always gave her good advice. As long as I could remember, my mom was always sick, and you could always find her home either talking to neighbors passing by our window or inviting people in for food or gossip.

My Brooklyn, My Way

    I remember the time when I was about six years old when Francis was in our kitchen talking to my mom. That day, without warning, nature called, and Francis had no choice but to use our bathroom. The problem was she weighed over three hundred pounds and took a mad dash to get to our toilet. Luck was not with Francis that day. She got stuck between the tub and the wall. My mom had to call the fire department to free her. She never made it, and I am sure you could imagine the mess that followed.

**My mom taking me out of the sock drawer
to get some fresh air (1941)**

Our Telephone

Our telephone had a party line, which meant you shared the phone with other families. Our phone number was Dickens 5-2364. You could not use the phone unless the other parties were off the line. The first thing you did when you had to make a call was pick up the phone and listen if somebody was talking. Then you had to wait for a dial tone and that could take up to five minutes. If you spoke too long, the other party would get on the phone telling you to get off already. There were many times you could hear them breathing, listening to your conversation.

The Public Phone

Our corner candy store on Amboy Street and Dumont Avenue was a meeting place for the kids from my block. If there was nobody on the street, which was seldom, you could always find a friend hanging out on the corner. It was owned by Sam Cohen, a heavy man with thick glasses. His wife and daughter, Arlene, helped him behind the soda fountain. Arlene was my age and always shared her candy with me, always having a handful in her pocket.

    You could find a candy store on just about every block in Brownsville. If you had some loose change in your pocket, you could always find something to buy. For two cents, you could find some chocolate, gum, or different candies. If you had a nickel or a dime, you could purchase a comic book or newspaper or even treat yourself to a malted or ice cream soda. I liked to buy candy cigarettes or waxed Coke-shaped plastic bottles with colored sugar water inside. There was a Seeburg jukebox that played 45 rpm records that would light up and spin with rainbow-colored lights. You could play three songs for a dime. In the back of the store were two tables with hard red leather bench seats. I preferred sitting at the counter watching Sam serve. Sam would tell you to go outside if you were not making a purchase or you finished your soda. In the back of his candy store was a public phone booth that had one phone. It had a long black telephone cord that would hang to the floor.

    Most families in the early '50s did not own phones. They would give out the candy store phone number if they had to be contacted. This gave my friends and me the opportunity to earn some extra money. My friends and I would listen for the phone to ring and would take turns answering. When we asked the party whom they wanted to speak to, we would ask the address and apartment number. That kid would leave the phone hanging and run out of the store to notify that person they had a phone call at Sam's. There were times I remember running up three flights of stairs because the buildings did not have a buzzer in the hallways. A tip was always given to that boy notifying them. I would save up those nickels for a lime rickey if it was a real hot day. But there were times I preferred a cherry soda or vanilla malted.

My friends from Amboy Street hanging out on the stoop (1956)

Family Planning

**My mom pregnant with Bruce but kept it a secret
(1944)**

When I first moved to Amboy Street, my youngest brother, Bruce, was not born. He came three years later. My eldest brother, Bob, was twelve years old, and Herb was ten. My zodiac sign is Virgo. I was born on September 12, 1941. My elder brother Herb was also born on September 12 but in 1931. We are exactly ten years apart. I figured out that having both of us born on the same date had to have been planned by my parents, probably on a cold day in January.

My brother Jack is three years older than me. When my younger brother Bruce was born, Jack became the middle child. My mom kept her pregnancy with Bruce a secret. Nobody knew she was pregnant until the day her water broke. My mom always wore a long house dress, better known as a *shmata*, so nobody knew she was pregnant. That included my father.

I guess the reason why my mom kept her pregnancy a secret was because her doctors told her because of her bad heart, it could be fatal to have a child but I guess she ignored the warning and didn't want anyone to know.

Sleeping

The strangest thing about our living arrangement was that since my father was a mailman and had to get up early to deliver the mail in Manhattan Beach, he had his own room. That left my mom and her five sons with one bedroom. We did make good use of the living room sofa that opened up into a bed. My two elder brothers shared their own bedroom. That left me, my mom, and my two brothers on the sofa. We were only able to fit if we lay in different positions. Sometimes when I woke up in the morning, our positions changed and my brother's feet were in my face. Today, people wake up with the smell of fresh brewed coffee; I woke up with the smell of sweaty feet. There is a Jewish word that describes this position when sleeping. It's called *suffussen*. There is no English word that describes this anomaly better.

When I got up in the morning, the first thing I would do was have my Rice Krispies cereal with homogenized milk. There were days when my mom wasn't feeling well so I ate the same brand of cereal for breakfast, lunch, and supper. I wanted to make it easy as possible for my mom so she could relax. She would lie down on her "rock" pillow which put her head straight up and that made it easier for her to breathe. We had a large floor fan that rotated the hot air which made her more comfortable while lying down on the bed.

During those years, parents would constantly give their children milk because it has vitamin D, which builds strong bones. In today's world, kids drink very little milk. Also, when my mother did cook, she would always say to finish everything because there are children staving in Europe. I would say, "Can we send my leftovers to them?" She would say, "No, finish what's on your plate."

My clothes that I wore from the prior day were the same clothes that were laid out for the next morning. It would be rolled up into a ball and placed on the chair, which made it easy for me to decide what to wear. These were the same clothes my brothers wore and outgrew. I don't remember ever buying new clothes. While my three elder brothers were growing out of their clothes, I always had something to wear. Sometimes, I had to wait an extra year because my brother Jack was next in line. But I didn't care; I knew that sooner or later, it would be mine. Being a happy child, if I had to wear my knickers and a striped T-shirt every day, that was also fine. If my trousers were too long, I would roll up the cuff. I remember rolling up my elder brothers' trousers about fivefold until it fit me. When I started to grow and got taller, I would unfold one cuff at a time. My pants always had holes in them. I think today's fashion has followed that trend because I see everyone wearing ripped jeans. I think that made me a trendsetter.

The next thing I would do in the morning was wash and brush my teeth in the kitchen sink since there was no washstand in our bathroom. I was very careful pushing the dirty dishes to the side of the sink. This way, while washing the dirt from my hands, I never touched the dirty dishes. If my brothers were all getting ready at the same time, I would have to wait in line to use the bathroom. My eldest brother, Bob, studied in the bathroom and we had to knock on the door to ask him to let us in. We were very careful not to get his books wet, knowing how young boys are. Our aim was pretty accurate which was probably because we were all good in sports and always took practice shots when we saw a hoop.

I remember my father's answer when I asked him why he had five sons. His answer was he always wanted to own a basketball team. When I asked my mom, "How come my brother Herb is exactly ten years older than me?" My mom would answer, "It was planned so when your brother was ten, rather than spend the money to buy him a toy, it was cheaper to have you for a gift."

The Blumberg Boys

The Blumberg Boys (1952)

Coming from a family of five boys, we were known as the Blumberg boys around the neighborhood. Since our ages were about three years apart from one another, every age group was friends with one of us. I had an Aunt Evie, my father's sister, who said my mom had five diamonds, but she always favored my eldest brother, Bob. She would say he was a perfect stone. I guess that meant that the rest of my brothers and I had many imperfections.

My friends and I would take long walks but never wander too far. There were times when we would find a stray dog and take the dog along as our chaperone. We tied a rope around the dog's neck and took him for the stroll in the area. Maybe it gave us confidence that we had a dog to protect us. But we had more fear of the dog attacking us than other kids in the area. As we walked the streets, we would always notice stray dogs and cats roaming around in packs. You would see them running in alleyways at a pretty fast speed. There was a boy on our block who we called Harvey the Cat Killer. The story goes that somebody saw him throwing a cat in the furnace in his building. We did keep our distance from Harvey, and so did the cats.

Amboy Street

I remember all my friends' names, and that goes back more than seventy years. I recall the games we played in the streets of Brooklyn. I just hope that these experiences will be preserved for future generations. In retrospect, they were not only my friends but also one big family that I had feelings and loyalty to. I knew everyone's nickname and their siblings' names. I guess the main reason was we lived in the streets longer than in our tenement houses. Brooklyn was what I call a utopia. Every morning I woke up, there was a smile on my face.

I feel that the world today would be a much better place if people had lived and experienced how life was during that era. Some people may look back and say they were tough years, but our parents taught us to show respect and that by working hard, you'll succeed. And especially, we were shown that there is much more to life than material things. Good health, family, and good friends were much more important. We were Brooklynites who grew up in a working-class atmosphere. Most of my friends called me Motchkee. Even today, my friend Mike Charney calls me that.

Growing up in Brownsville may not seem something one would brag about, but it makes me proud to say those words. Brownsville was a special place in my life. I cherish all these memories, and without any doubt, these were great years of my life. Without making any changes, I would live my childhood days all over again. I understand that throughout Brooklyn, there are neighborhoods with its individual charm. When Brooklynites think of their upbringing, it brings smiles to their faces. There were always kids who were ready to play any type of game. The streets were safe, and our parents thought nothing that we stayed out late. Remember, this was a time after the Amboy Dukes and before Mike Tyson, who was born and raised on Amboy Street.

I do not think that Amboy Street was unique. There were many areas in Brooklyn where kids witnessed similar experiences growing up. I am sure most Brooklynites will relate to the many different stories from my memoir. I feel fortunate that I remember it so well and have been given the opportunity to put it down on paper and share with my readers.

I'm sure when you visualize the block where you grew up, there were probably many stores and dwellings you might recall. Just on my street alone, there were about ten store owners who knew me by my first name. If my family needed something, they would trust us and let us pay when we had the money. Whatever you wanted to do was a short walk away. We were fortunate to live within walking distance to Pitkin Avenue, which was the main shopping area in Brownsville.

Pitkin Avenue had banks, movie theaters, and just about any store imaginable. If you needed a suit, there was Penrod's or Richfield Clothes. I remember as a child looking in the window display from Abe Stark, who sold men's clothes. If you needed a new pair of shoes, there was Eppy and Eppy. For excellent Chinese food, there was Wuhan's Chinese restaurant. For sporting goods, there was Rimberg. The Kishke King on Pitkin Avenue had the best ten-inch hot dogs. If you were a coconut lover (which I am not), you would always see Coconut Jim, who owned a coconut stand that specialized selling coconut icees. He was a real character, always wearing fatigues and a safari helmet, always with a hatchet in his hand chopping pieces of coconut and selling it by the piece. I am not a coconut lover, but people would line up to buy "a lovely piece of coconut all standing in a row."

**Our apartment at 260 Amboy Street
above the garbage cans**

My Mother

My mom's maiden name was Frieda Halperin. She was born on the lower east side on Broome Street. Her father's name was Harry and her mother was Rebecca. They both came here from Russia. She was born in 1907 and died in 1969 at the age of sixty-two. She was the eldest, having three brothers and a sister. With a bad heart, she lived longer than most doctors believed. In retrospect, knowing how much in today's world we have learned about her heart condition with replacement of valves and heart pacers, she may have lived a lot more years.

My mom spoke mostly English but she also understood and spoke Yiddish. She had a very good voice, and her favorite song was "My Yiddishe Mama." When my mother had a good day she would cook a hot dinner. Friday night was always chicken. I recall my dad going to the slaughterhouse picking out a kosher chicken. Since the chicken was freshly killed, I recall my mother cleaning off some of the feathers and cleaning out the inside. If it was a female chicken, many times she would pull out unborn little eggs. She called them eyerlekh which were not-fully- developed chicken eggs. I recall my my mom placing them in our soup. They were small hard yellow yolks that had a sweet and delicate flavor. My mom would eat Chinese food and other non kosher food but she insisted on kosher chicken. While the food was cooking, she would sit by the window leaning on her pillow, talking to people passing by. Since we did not leave the house that often, many of our relatives would stop by on weekends without an invitation. My mom always entertained them with food and drink.

She had rheumatic heart disease and was always on medication called digitalis. She had about five heart attacks that I knew of. Each time, doctors gave up hope but by some divine miracle, she pulled through. Her regular doctor's name was Dr. Grosoff. There was a time my younger brother Bruce, who was an infant at that time, had to be placed in a "home" because there was nobody around to take care of him.

There were many times we had to call an ambulance to take my mom to the hospital. I remember standing by the door as a little boy crying as she was wheeled out on a stretcher. As they put her in the ambulance, I would always think, *Is she coming home?* I would pray to God that he watched over her and have her return back to Amboy Street.

I remember running down the street to a Dr. Goldsmith to come to our house for a house call. My mom was having a hard time breathing. He came right over with his black medical bag. I remember listening to him at the door talking to my father and telling him how sick my mom was. My dad would pay him at the door. One incident that I recall, was he told my dad the charge was five dollars. I heard my father bargaining with him, and he lowered his price to three dollars because my father told him he only had to walk across the street.

My mom looking out the window on Amboy Street (1944)

Cooking

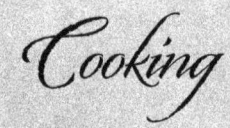

My mom was considered a *balabusta*, which is a Jewish term for a great homemaker. She was a pretty good cook but not perfect. She never timed how long food should be cooked, never measured the amount of salt or pepper, and surely never followed any recipes. But she did make some good dishes. She did have a habit of overcooking some of the meats. That may be the reason I only order medium rare when eating out. She did make a mean flanken (which is strips of beef cut across the bone from the chuck end of the short ribs). The leftovers would be put in a mushroom-barley soup that was out of this world. The aroma alone would make my mouth salivate.

My mom cooked lots of different meals that she inherited from her mom. One dish that comes to mind was noodles and cottage cheese, which most probably started out as deconstructed kugel. It was commonly eaten across Eastern Europe. In Yiddish, my mom called this dish *lokshen*. She would make this dish with noodles and cottage cheese; sometimes, she would alter it with the addition of fried onions or sour cream or butter. I could still taste those fried onions right now.

My mom never went to culinary school. She never followed a written recipe. She cooked from memory, and she never used any measuring device. She would shake the salt or pepper in a pot, talking at the same time and not realizing how much she used. Not everything she cooked came out tasting divine. But there is one dish she made that always comes to mind close to the holidays - that's Mom's split pea soup with frankfurters.

I recall as a child watching my mom put all types of ingredients in a pot, mashing the peas and adding carrots, salt, pepper, and garlic. Then she would add the sliced frankfurters she boiled separately. She would constantly stir and then let it simmer for an hour. The aroma was all through our apartment, and it smelled enticing. It made my mouth water, and I couldn't wait for that first taste of her thick pea soup.

For more than the past half century, I have tried many variations of split pea soup. I have gone to some of the best restaurants and had this soup prepared by the best chefs in the world. But none compared with my mom's split pea soup. All these chefs can learn a lesson from her pea soup. The only problem is she never wrote down the recipe.

I do miss the taste of that soup, but most of all, I miss seeing her in the kitchen preparing that delicacy.

My Father

His name was Irving Blumberg. He was born on the lower east side of Manhattan on December 27, 1907. His father, Samuel, and mother, Anna, arrived here from Eastern Europe and married in New York. He died in 1990 at the age of eighty-two. He attended Boys High School in Brooklyn. He retired from the U.S. Post Office after working for more than forty years as a letter carrier. His route was Brighton Beach and Manhattan Beach.

My father went to sleep early every night so he could get to the post office to sort and deliver the mail. He never missed a day of work. He believed in the motto *"Neither snow nor rain nor heat nor gloom of night stays these couriers from the swift completion of their appointed rounds."*

If a snowstorm was in the forecast, he would park his car six blocks away to be under the (el) train tracks so he would have less snow to shovel and pull right out.

His nickname was Kelly. I would ask him why a Jewish person would come up with a name like Kelly. He told me that at Christmastime, his Christmas gift was double the amount. These rich judges, lawyers, and professionals whom he delivered mail to in their big, gorgeous mansions in Manhattan Beach would put in an envelope four dollars instead of two dollars. He would say; "With a name like Kelly, you do much better than with a name like Irving."

We had a close relationship with each other. When he came home from work, we would go to the supermarket together. He had a fabulous mind and was terrific in math, and as he would place items in the cart, his mind would be adding each item in his head. When the clerk started to ring up each item on the cash register, he already knew what the total would be, including tax.

I remember one time there was a twenty-cent difference. My father asked the clerk to ring it all over again. Yes, he was right, and being frugal, for the next two weeks, he would brag to everyone how he saved twenty cents.

I think my father always had it in his blood to be an entrepreneur. He came home one day from work and told us he was not leaving the post office, but he invested in another business. I asked him what he intended to do. He said he bought a vending machine route. He noticed an ad in the newspaper about a person who was retiring and wanted to sell his accounts, along with his vending machines.

I do not recall what he paid, but I told him I would help him on the route traveling to different parts of Brooklyn to help him fill up the nuts, gum, and charms inserted in capsules that would hold small objects. He serviced a few bars on Church Avenue, where he had cashew machines. That was a quarter machine, and every week, it was loaded with quarters. Since these people would drink, they also loved cashews nuts. There was a drugstore named Silver Rods on Church Avenue that had a vending machine on the outside wall. It never failed to be either vandalized or broken. I gave it a nickname "Old Faithful."

My father started to expand and took on other locations. He even had some locations on Pitkin Avenue. When I got home from junior high school, I would drive with him to these locations, help fill up the machines, and count the money. He would walk in with a scale that weighed the money. The store owner would get a commission on the total count.

He would buy his merchandise on Empire Boulevard near Ebbets Field at a store called Shoenfelds. I remember the machines were always breaking down, and my father kept the extra parts and nuts and charms all in his bedroom. His bedroom became so crowded that you couldn't walk in the room. It had a disheveled appearance, and rodents started to appear.

The business name was Irveda, which was short for Irving and Frieda. My mom made him get rid of the business because it became out of control. I just wish we kept some of those peanut machines because today they sell for hundreds of dollars each. That's without the worms.

My dad delivering the mail in Manhattan Beach (1946)

Bob

Bob, the eldest of the brothers, always showed an interest in school. He was the studious son and always stressed the value of education. He would give me and my brothers advice and help us with our schoolwork. To get away from all the commotion and noise in our apartment, he would take his books into the bathroom, lock the door, and study. He played football for Tilden during his high school years.

Our apartment on Amboy Street was like a subway stop. There were always people going in and out. My mom would take her pillow, leaving it on the windowsill, and talk to the people passing by. There were times when she would invite them in our apartment and feed them. I remember some unusual people in conversation with my mom. It seemed to be the main spot where people would stop and talk about the latest news story.

There was a distant relative named Nathan. I have no idea how he was related to us, but my mom said he was part of the family. I never asked questions, but I think he was related on my father's side. He was about four feet tall and always had a trumpet in his hand. I think his job was to play for people in the alleyways, where tenants would wrap change in a tissue and toss it down to him. He would stop by every once in a while for a hot meal my mom prepared for him. He was scary looking but compared with Annie Hunk, he was a Clark Gable.

Then there was a gal we called Annie Hunk. I have no idea how she became a fixture in our apartment. I was only about seven years old when I first noticed her. My guess is my mother started a conversation when she passed by our window. Since my mom was ill, Annie would do certain chores around our home and care for my younger brother Bruce. I don't recall money exchanging hands, but she would sit at our kitchen table, have coffee, and eat from the cookie jar that sat on our kitchen table. Every time right before she took a taste of that cookie, she would smell it. She became friendly with my mom. My mom had a manner of being a good listener and would say things that encouraged people. Annie Hunk was a person who needed lots of encouragement.

My oldest brother Robert (Bob) knew Annie better than my other brothers because he was about fifteen when she came into the picture. Decades later, he wrote his memoir describing his experience with the Hunk. This true story takes place in the late '40s on Amboy Street in Brownsville. I did not know his memoir ever existed until he showed it to me about a year ago. It gives you a good idea of what went on in our apartment on Amboy Street during those years.

Bob studying in a classroom instead of the bathroom (1945)

Annie Hunk

by Robert Blumberg

She was an Amazon. In those early days, we called any woman over 6 foot tall, an Amazon (and any girl under 5 foot, a Pygmy). To my family, she was Annie Hunk. Today, the word "Hunk" would apply to a Tom Selleck or a Don Johnson. Annie wasn't that kind of a "hunk" at all. She was more like a "chunk," a 6 foot, 1 inch, 250 pound Amazon, with brown, stringy, oily, matted hair, two missing front teeth, unruly, overflowing breasts, and legs that were all knees.

Annie Hunk came before TV. She was the news of the day, the morning cartoon, the afternoon "soap," the long running sitcom. Sometimes, she would show up with a bag of bagels, before anyone was awake. Other times she would tap on the door in the middle of the night, just back from a date with Pacey, her runty, crater-faced boyfriend. Annie was the first "loose woman" I had ever known. I knew that she was doing something dirty with Pacey, but I didn't really know what "dirty" was all about. At 15, I was too busy playing punchball or swimming by day, and watching over mom at night. Now, I can only visualize a rather horsey Amazon, and her jockey-like paramour. I guess I accepted their relationship at face value. If Annie Hunk were around today. If she were still among the living, she would be the quintessential bag lady. Pacey would be found opening and closing a neighborhood OTB, or among the losers at Belmont, running drugs, or selling condoms to high schoolers.

It was a Sunday morning, sometime in the mid-forties. Someone was knocking at the door. Mom had had a good night. She hadn't wheezed. She hadn't lost her breath, nor awakened fighting for precious air, complaining about piercing pains in the region of her heart. There was no need to call Doctor Grosoff, nor an Emergency Ambulance from Union Hospital.

My Brooklyn, My Way

We slept. All of us. My youngest brother, Bruce slept with mom on the foldaway couch. I slept with Herb, and Jack bunked with Martin. Dad was tucked away in his room. The light was still on and the Donnelly stamp catalogue was opened to British New Guinea. The green and white bedspread had not been removed. Hundreds of gummed stamp hinges were all over the floor. Dad was in that heavy sleep which comes in the last few hours before we awake. Sunday, Dad would sleep until nine. That was five hours better than his six day ritual of rising at four so that he could get to the Post Office by 5:30.

"Who is it?" I asked. I had climbed over Herb trying not to wake him up and tiptoed to the kitchen door. I didn't want to wake Herb. He'd had a big basketball game last night against the Belvederes at the Betsy Head Center, and was bound to be exhausted. The linoleum was like ice. "It's Annie Fiegler," a familiar voice answered. I opened the door, but did not undo the security chain. "Annie Hunk, what are you doing here? What time is it anyway?"

"Let me in, Robert," Annie begged. "It's about 7:30. Pacey just dropped me off. I bought some delicious bagels."

"Annie," I pleaded, as I opened the door, "everyone is sleeping. Thank God. Mom had a good night. Dad is sound asleep. All the boys are sleeping. Why don't you sit in the kitchen? Have a bagel. Make some coffee. I'm going back to bed Annie, don't make a peep. It's Sunday morning."

"Pacey's going to jail," she said with her head down. I looked at her. She was wearing a blue cardigan sweater with only the top button closed. Her light blue print dress was her "going-out" dress. She wore open-toed high high heels, which made her six foot five, at least. When she sat down on the kitchen chair she removed her shoes. Her stockings had more runs than the New York Yankees, and she yielded a scent that could not be squelched by her cheap perfume.

"What do you mean, Annie?" I said. "What do you mean that Pacey is going to jail?" "He punched a cop on Friday night," Annie answered. "And he just knows that the entire 73rd Precinct will be after him."

"So why don't he just give himself up," I suggested. "Let him explain himself, get a lawyer, and they'll leave him alone until the trial. Annie, why did Pacey punch a cop?"

"He didn't know the guy was a cop," Annie replied. "Pacey was playing craps just behind Victor's Drugstore on Bristol Street, and the game was busted. Bosco, Eppy, Pigeon and Moose ran and so did Pacey, when this tall guy, with no uniform, no badge, nothin', asked Pacey who he was. He grabbed Pacey by his collar and Pacey punched him in the mouth. Pacey thinks that he knocked out his tooth. Moose told Pacey last night that the guy was a cop, a new plainclothes from the 86th in Midwood. Pacey is scared suit. If he goes back to jail, they'll throw away the key. I've got to talk to your Uncle Lefty." She is crying. Her heavy makeup began to run, leaving only her large crimson lips to catch the streams of black mascara. "Lefty can help Pacey," she insisted. "He pays the cops off to let him run his poolroom. Everybody knows it. Robert, what time will Lefty be here today?"

"Annie, how do I know? I don't know these things. I'm going back to sleep."

Mom walked into the kitchen, which was two steps from the living room where she slept with little Bruce. "I thought that was you, Annie," Mom said. "What are you doing here so early? What did I hear you say about Pacey? He's in jail? Good, I told you to dump that midget years ago. He can't be trusted. He'll never provide for you. You're a good girl, Annie. What do you see in that punk?" Mom walked into the bathroom which was just off the kitchen and shortly reappeared to wash herself and brush her teeth. Our one and only bathroom had no sink and we washed and dishwashed in the same basin.

"Frieda," Annie said, "Pacey is nice to me. He buys me things. He's got a car and drives me to the city sometimes on Saturday. Here, look at this bracelet, Frieda."

"It's a fake," Mom said. "If it costs 25 cents in Woolworth, it's a lot. Annie, you're a nice girl. Get rid of Pacey, let him go to jail. My neighbor, Tessie, has a handsome brother. She wants him to get married. He's a plumber and works steady. I'm going to make the introduction. You'll lose some weight and fix your two front teeth. I'll wash and comb your hair. You'll see Annie, I'll work everything out for you."

"But Frieda," Annie came back at Mom, "you've been telling me about Tessie's brother for three years. Meanwhile, I can't let Pacey go to jail. What time will Lefty be here today?"

"Maybe at three or three-thirty, after the bets are all in. He comes every Sunday with Esther and the three boys. They eat us out of house and home. And when he's here who knows he's here? He listens to the radio in the living room and all he talks about is odds, shmods, points, shmoints, football, shmootball. They're going to go after Lefty one day and shoot him up. He's mixed up with the wrong people. He's playing with fire. Annie, you don't need Lefty, and you don't need Pacey."

Annie wept openly. Mom walked over to the range, lit a match and began to make some A&P 8:o'clock coffee. "These bagels smell good, Annie," she said, "how many are there?"

"Twenty-six," Annie smiled. "I got two free!"

Mom said, "When the boys get up, they'll have your bagels with cream cheese which I bought at Braverman's just yesterday. I'll save the rest for company. Annie, would you do me a favor and run down to Braverman's? Fill up this pitcher with milk and ask Ben to give us a half pound of butter. I'll need it for the eggs. And charge it!"

While Annie was gone, my brothers Jack and Marty wandered, sleepy-eyed into the kitchen. Neither one wore slippers. "Gee this floor is cold, what's for breakfast, Mom?" Martin asked. Martin was already wearing his suspender knickers and striped polo shirt. I think that Mom dressed Marty in this outfit on Memorial Day, and he wore it until Labor Day. Jack was the family's Gerber baby. Fat cheeks, always smiling, always whistling or singing. Mom would dress Jacky everyday with a pressed shirt and corduroy pants in summer and winter.

"Let's play one on one," Martin suggested to Jack. Martin ran into my bedroom and was back instantly with a rolled up sock. He slid a bent hanger into the top of the kitchen door to form a basketball rim. Suddenly, the game began. Martin provided the play-by-play.

"Marty dribbles to the circle, fakes out Jack, sets . . . and whoosh, two points. Jack gets ready for a hook shot. Marty has his hands way up, Jack hooks. No good. Martin dribbles back to half court. The great playmaker is in action. Sets. Goood! 4 nothing!"

No sooner had the game begun, when Herb and Bruce stepped into the kitchen. "How do you feel, Mom?" Herb asked. "Thank God, I slept. I think that the Digitalis (Doctor Grosoff prescribed) is working OK. Why don't you wash up? Annie will be here in a minute with some milk and butter. She brought us some bagels. We'll have it with some scrambled eggs. Close Daddy's door. Let him sleep. And tell Robert to hurry up and get dressed before Annie Hunk returns."

A typical day on Amboy Street written by my brother Bob. Annie Hunk was just one of many characters that were invited in our home.

Herb

Herb would spend time watching sports on TV. He also loved music and loved to sing along with his favorite artists. Since we had a big record collection, he would play his favorite records. He loved the sounds of the big bands. I remember when he went on a date, my job was to hand him his clothes, which he called his "attire." His favorite song was "I Cover the Waterfront," by Billie Holiday. He played basketball for Tilden High during his high school years.

My brother Herb, who was five feet seven inches, also played basketball for a local team called the Rimsters. He had a great "set shot." Most kids nowadays never even heard of a set shot. You shot the ball with two hands with your feet never leaving the ground. He was also a skilled dribbler and playmaker.

I was about eight years old and watched him play at the BBC (Brownsville Boys Club) or the HES (Hebrew Educational Society), and, yes also Betsy Head Park which had an indoor basketball court. As a little boy, I recall watching exciting basketball games. Some of the players on his team were Boris Nashamkin, Solly Walker, Duvi Hartman, and Al Turtz. They all lived in Brownsville and were all-star quality. My brother's nickname was Hebel. They played against an all-black team called the ViceRoys, many of whom in later years played professional basketball. A few players I remember watching were James "Dutch" Sparrow, Danny Cullen, and Gerry Harper. All were very fast and always had fast breaks bringing the ball down court.

One year, when Herb was about 16 years old he played in Madison Square Garden for the city championship. It was scheduled for a Saturday afternoon. Duvi (one of their top players) was religious and did not travel on the Sabbath. They were sure to lose big if he did not play. For some unknown reason, he showed up on that Saturday. The game score was up and then down to the final seconds, and they lost by one point. Duvi played great, and everyone on the team was very proud of his performance. But nobody asked him how he got there. The rumor was that he walked from Brooklyn since he would never ride in the subway or drive in a car on Saturday. It became a puzzle, and nobody asked or got an answer.

In 1998, I went with my wife, Maxine, along with my brothers Bob and Herb and their wives to a vacation in Israel to celebrate the establishment of the state's fiftieth year of independence. The main speaker was a Mr. Hartman. We had no idea this was the same Duvid Hartman my brother lost contact with for over fifty years. Duvid Hartman dedicated his life to Israel. Yes, a Jewish boy from Brooklyn became a big mocha.

We were in a big hall, and there were many prominent speakers. Then they announced David Hartman. After his speech, Herb realized this was the Hartman he played basketball with. It was a beautiful sight. They recognized each other and then hugged, and you could see the tears and the warmth on their faces. They embraced again, and Herb asked him the question he never knew the answer. "Duvi, how did you get to Madison Square Garden? Did you really walk from Brooklyn to the Garden?" He finally heard the truth. Duvi answered that he stayed in the city the night before and walked a few blocks to the Garden. I'll always remember that day. They then embraced the same way they did 50 years prior when they played on the Rimsters basketball team.

David Hartman was an American Israeli leader and philosopher of contemporary Judaism; founder of the Shalom Hartman Institute in Jerusalem, Israel; and a Jewish author. He was born on September 11, 1931, in Brooklyn, a day before my brother Herb. Rabbi David Hartman passed away on February 10, 2013.

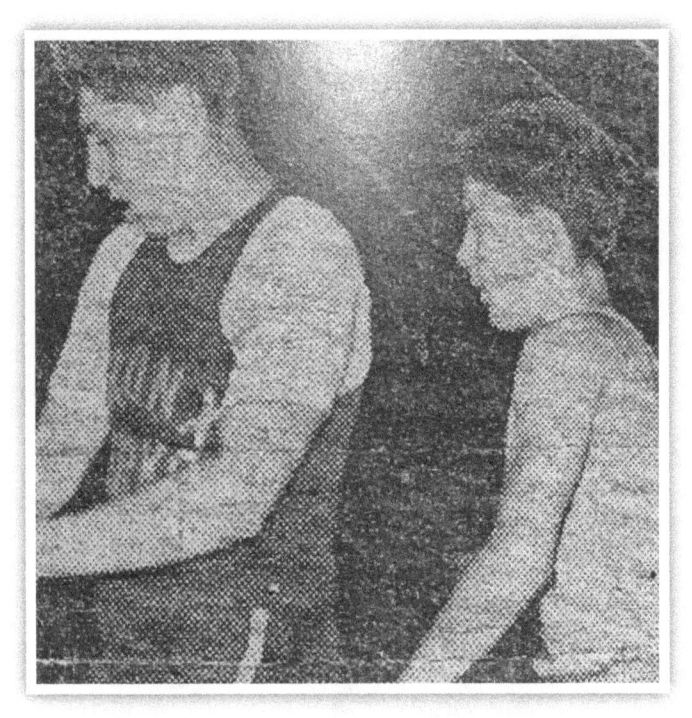

Herb playing basketball in Madison Square Garden for the City Championship (1947)

Jack

Jack sitting in car (1952)

Jack had a baseball league that was played on our linoleum kitchen floor. He would take nine playing cards from the Brooklyn Dodgers, place them in their positions in his make-believe baseball field, and then take an opposing team, like the Yankees, and set up their lineup. He would make a small round ball from rubber bands and yell out, "Play ball!" He would throw the ball in the air and take a swing with the card, and then after the swing, he would announce the game out loud. If he got a hit, he would make noise and sounds of fans cheering. He kept score and records, and at the end of the season, there was a World Series. The fans in stands would cheer or boo depending on who was up.

I remember standing in the outfield near our bathroom watching the game. He did make it exciting, and I would watch the game for a few innings. Sometimes, he would take a swing, and the playing card he used as a bat would rip. He even called balls and strikes. You may think that Jack was nuts, but when I started to cheer and root for a player, I was nuttier than him.

He had some really good cards like Duke Snider and a 1952 Topps Mickey Mantle card. One day, he took a swing with the Mantle card and connected with the rolled-up rubber band ball. He hit a tremendous blast that went over the kitchen table and landed in the kitchen sink. Yes, it was a home run, but the card ripped and ended up in the garbage. Years later, I realized it was Mantle's rookie card. In today's market, it would be worth tens of millions of dollars. In retrospect, if Mantle struck out and he kept that card in mint condition, Jack would have been on easy street, instead of Amboy Street.

Bruce

One activity that took place in our kitchen was playing basketball. My brother Bruce and I would roll up a sock and make believe we were dribbling a basketball. We loved basketball, and to score, you would throw the sock on the kitchen table in a cookie jar. The cookies were never taken out of the jar, and his dirty socks intermingled with the cookies. I think that was the reason Annie Hunk thought they were so tasty and took a sniff before she ate them.

We dribbled by moving our hands up and down. We kept score and took foul shots. If you did not dribble, you were called for walking. I remember one time Bruce used one of his soggy socks that just came off his foot as the basketball. He took a shot that I deflected, and sock stuck to the ceiling. We had to call time-out to get it down with a broomstick.

Bruce also loved baseball and played in the Little League, Babe Ruth League, and at Thomas Jefferson High School.

So as you can see, being a Blumberg boy was something special. We had a strong bond and upbringing that kept us together. If we were in groups or just being alone, our personalities drew other people wanting to be around us and experience life in such a positive manner.

My younger brother Bruce is saying he can't wait any longer and wants my shirt. He has been waiting three years and now it's his turn. (1952)

Batboy for a Day

The date was May 1, 1957, and the Brooklyn Dodger Organization was running a contest for young children. The winner would become the Dodger batboy for a day. There were thousands of entries not only from Brooklyn but also throughout New York State. My younger brother Bruce tied with another boy, Joey, for first prize.

The entry had to be one hundred words or less about why you wanted to be a Dodger batboy for a day. My brother's went like this:

> "I want to be a Dodger batboy not only because I love baseball, not only because I love the Dodgers even more, and not because it would be the most exciting day of my life, but I guess the most important reason is because I am a boy, and what boy wouldn't want to be a Dodger batboy even for a day?"

The other boy, Joey, shared first place with my younger brother Bruce. I remember one line from his entry: "If you don't succeed at first, try for second base."

What a fantastic day it turned out to be at the ballgame. My whole family was invited to sit behind the Dodgers' dugout and watch my brother hand the bats to players like Roy Campanella, Duke Snyder, Gil Hodges, and even Pee Wee Reese. Even my mom came without her pillow to witness her son on national TV and be announced to the thousands of spectators. The sun was shining, the Dodgers won and my family proudly sang "Take Me Out to the Ballgame."

My brother was given a Dodger uniform, a new pair of socks, a picture album of him with the team, a video and a signed autographed baseball, and the opportunity to meet and greet the greatest baseball team ever - the 1957 Brooklyn Dodgers. It was just great watching him hand the bats to the players, slapping them high fives when getting a hit. He also handed the umpires new baseballs.

Some of the other players who were on the field during the game were Don Drysdale, Junior Gilliam, and Sandy Koufax, and Don Newcombe pitched and won.

How about that for a day out to the ballpark? Who needed peanuts and crackerjacks? It was a day I'll never forget, and I am sure my brother Bruce felt the same way.

Sitting behind the Brooklyn Dodger dugout at Ebbets Field after my brother Bruce won a contest "why I want to be Brooklyn Dodger batboy for a day." (1957)

Trek to Canarsie

I remember a cousin of one of my friends, Mendy, who would come to Amboy Street for a visit. His name was Harvey Cantor. He was two years older than us. That was unusual because there were so many kids your age to hang out with and most kids only hung out with their age group, but Harvey wanted to be with us younger boys. One day, I recall Harvey was going to take us on a hike to Canarsie. He told our group of six to follow him, and we started our trek. He told us that we would see an ocean with boats and people fishing. It sounded exciting. We even found a stray dog on the way that joined us on this adventure. We all picked up large tree branches on the way to help us keep balance.

On our way to Canarsie, which was at least five miles, we passed streets I never knew existed because we never strayed that far from Amboy Street. When we approached Canarsie, we noticed a row of Quonset huts. They were built for U.S. veterans who returned to NYC after WWII. These barracks were built by the government so the returning soldiers with families had housing.

We finally got to the pier and noticed the ocean. It was a whole different world looking out toward Jamaica Bay. The ocean looked much cleaner than Betsy Head Pool. We watched the fishermen unload the fish off the boats. When our leader, Harvey, told us it was getting dark, we returned back to Amboy Street. I would guess we were away for about seven hours. When I got home and saw my mom looking out the window, she said, "Did you eat your cereal today?" I just told her I forgot. I was too busy. My mom never asked me where I was for seven hours.

We never thought of crime and had no fear of staying out late. Life was worry free. In today's world, there would have been 911 calls with police

My Brooklyn, My Way

searching the area with SWAT teams looking for six missing boys. Oh, how the times have really changed.

In the winter, we would trek to East New York Avenue to Lincoln Terrace Park. There was a very steep hill, and we would go speeding down the hill on roller skates. When there was snow on the ground, we would go down that same hill with our sleds. We never wore helmets or any gear for protection. In retrospect, we could have gotten badly hurt. I guess we were just lucky.

At that time, my friends were into darts. These darts were about five inches long with a sharp point. We would throw the darts at a target on a tree to see who got the closest. We would also toss it high in the air. One time, the dart came down and landed in my foot. It was in really deep. I just pulled it out, wiped the blood, and continued playing. I never told my mom about the incident. It took about six months to heal, and then the hole finally closed.

A stray dog on Amboy Street (1951)

Grocery Shopping

The corner grocery store was where my mom would send me shopping. It was on the same block on which I lived, so I never had to cross the street. I remember reading the list my mom gave me, always including a Silvercup bread and a quart of homogenized milk. If there was an item on my list that I couldn't read, the grocer read it for me. I remember him using a long stick that would claw some boxes that were high on the shelves to get an item down. I never gave him any money, but the grocer would write everything I got on a brown paper bag, and then he would enter it in his book. On Fridays, when my dad got paid, he would settle the bill.

Compared with nowadays, it was so much easier to shop. Today, I can't even put my credit card chip in the right way. Now we have a new law in Suffolk County - if you forget to bring in your own shopping bags, you get charged. I keep forgetting to bring my wife's shopping list; now, how am I going to remember to bring shopping bags into the supermarket?

I just wish that corner grocery store would come back. I miss that personal relationship I had with the person behind the counter. Not only did he know my name, but he was also able to read my mom's handwriting. He even knew how to add using a pencil. Who needs plastic bags anyway? Bring back those paper bags.

Icebox

Before there were refrigerators, I remember having an icebox. The food was kept cold by having ice delivered to our apartment and put in a unit that held the ice. Every few days we would get a delivery of ice to replace the ice that melted. Our seltzer men were Al Pectker, and his son Larry. I remember watching them carry a dozen bottles of seltzer up three flights of steps. They were always out of breath.

    I was about thirteen years old, and on hot summer nights, my friends and I would take a walk around the block. Since nobody had air-conditioning, it was a way to cool off before bedtime. When in the house, my brothers and I would keep cool with our rotating fan. We would hold ice cubes in front of the fan to get a cool breeze. When the ice cubes melted, we would take turns by chopping another piece off a big block of ice we kept in our icebox. I know in today's world, we all have air conditioners. Usually, they break down on the hottest day. We did not have to worry; our ice was always cold. I remember on really hot nights, we slept at "tar beach" - that was what we called our roof. We would place a sheet on the roof and go to sleep, always remembering not to turn over or sleepwalk. Since we lived on the ground floor, we were not as fortunate as some of our neighbors who slept on their fire escapes.

Betsy Head Pool

I was fortunate to live a few blocks away from Betsy Head Pool. On a hot summer's day it was a great place to cool off. During those times I was able to enter the pool before 10:00 a.m. without a chaperone. That was called "free shift," but after 10:00 a.m. there was an entrance fee of ten cents, still a bargain, but I always went free shift so I wouldn't have to ask my mom for a dime. Walking into the entrance, the boys were to the right and girls to the left. When you walked in, there were long benches where you changed your clothes. There was a long counter with men giving out keys for a locker, which you tied around your foot or hand. I remember they collected your shoes, and you were handed a paper bag to put your clothes in and place in your locker. You could then use that bag to take home your wet bathing suit. The key was used to put your belongings in the lockers in the back, where there were showers and a bathroom. I recall having to walk through an infested foot pond that supposedly cleaned your feet while entering the pool area. I am sure many people walking through this fungus infested water picked up athlete's foot.

The pool was more than a block long and was next to a smaller pool with a sixteen-foot-high diving board. Many kids would jump or dive in and brag they jumped off the high board. The big pool had two islands in the middle of the pool. I always stayed in the area that was about four feet high. The other end was like a beach, and as you entered the pool, the water kept getting deeper. with no waves.

Since we lived on the ground floor of a three story building, there was always somebody passing by our window. When my mom noticed a friend passing, she would ask them to throw my lunch over the fence into the pool area. I recall a friend throwing my lunch a little to far and it landed in the pool. I took it out of the brown paper bag, ate it and never complained because it seemed like the chlorine gave it a better flavor and I finished the soggy sandwich. There were many days that I would eat my lunch and dinner at the pool and I stayed at the pool until dusk.

Outside the pool, there were big filters that would pump the chlorine into the pool. At night, we would sit on these filters because it blew out cool air that was refreshing. I would sit there debating with my friends who the best players were on the Brooklyn Dodgers. In the winter when the water was drained out of the pool, it was turned into softball courts. There was a balcony where people would sit and watch the softball games. Many home runs were hit over the balcony.

It was a rough area, and I do not recall much security. I remember when swimming in the pool, many of my friends had their bathing suits stolen. We had to throw them a towel so they could cover up. At the end of the day, when we left the pool area, we would exchange the keys for our shoes. A foolproof system, I never forgot my shoes.

This was how thousands of Brooklynites spent their summer days in Brownsville. Who needs day camps? Who needed air-conditioning? What I needed was an extra bathing suit in case mine got stolen.

Today, the park is still operating with some changes. It was named after a wealthy British immigrant named Betsy Head in 1915. She left $190.000 in her will to build Betsy Head recreational facility. The modern-day park contains a playground, recreation fields, and a bathhouse, which is situated on over 10 acres of land.

In 2008, the New York City Preservation Commission designated the Betsy Head Play area a landmark, the first In Brooklyn. In 2016, the playground was renovated for $5 million dollars and this year $30 million dollars will be allocated for further improvements over the next few years. Betsy Head Park has been serving the community for over 100 years.

Today Betsy Head is free to all who want to use the facility. Everybody is welcome but you must wear a bathing suit to get in. You must be 16 years of age or older unless accompanied by an adult. Everyday during the summer it is opened from 11AM to 3PM and the second shift from 4 to 7PM. You cannot bring any electronics, newspapers or any food into the pool area. I think the rule was changed when they found out 60 years prior my mom was having food thrown over the fence. It's hard for me to believe in today's world how they could control not having phones in the pool area.

My Brooklyn, My Way

They tell the patrons to make sure they have a sturdy combination lock to keep their electronics and valuables safe, so when you swim, your belongings are secure. They supply unlimited sunscreen which is free to all. They also say to leave your valuables at home which is a big change from what I remember in the early 50's. The only item that was stolen was your bathing suit, nobody had cell phones.

Betsy Head Pool

Chinatown

About every two months on a Sunday, my mom and dad would take us to Chinatown to a restaurant called Joy Garden. They would ask me and my brothers if we want to "eat Chinese." Joy Garden had the best food and was one of the best restaurants that I remember from my childhood. It was located at 57 Mott Street near Pell, which was a narrow street that was just wide enough for one car to pass at a time but was considered the main thoroughfare.

You had to walk up a flight of stairs to the second floor. I remember my mom would have to rest at the top of each step just to catch her breath. The food was delicious, and the prices were cheap. When you got to the top landing, I recall a big sign inside reading, "Please feel free to inspect our kitchen." At the time, people did question the cleanliness of Asian restaurants. But my dad always pointed out that we should look at how many Chinese people were eating there and that's how we would know it was a good restaurant, not realizing it was in the heart of Chinatown.

We would always start with the soup that was a mixture of egg drop and wonton and then the chow mein and chop suey, spareribs, and ending with shrimp with lobster sauce. I remember one time we ordered lobster Cantonese style. At the end of the meal, my brother told me to take the claws home, which I put in a bag. I do not remember the total bill, but I would guess for my whole family it was in the ten-dollar range, that included the tip.

The next day, my brother Jack told me to bring the lobster shells to school. He told me they were for "show and tell" day. So that was what I did. I went up in front of the class and opened the bag. I pulled out a lobster claw and told the class, "This is the meal I ate yesterday. At one time, this lobster was alive and swam in the ocean. Now it is dead, so I ate it." Mrs. Dubin loved my presentation, and I received two stars. I remember passing the claws around the class. I still don't know why, but I took the lobster shells home after show and tell. I still don't remember if I threw them in the garbage or placed them under my bed. I'm not sure, but it still may be there.

Catskills

Everything was concentrated on our family and friends. Money was an issue, but we always had food on the table. We may have been poor, but we never knew it. I do recall a few summers going to the Catskills mountains. My dad very rarely made reservations, so we stayed in different hotels, bungalows, as well as some cook-a-lanes, wherever he found the best deal. I remember staying in a place one night and the next night staying somewhere else.

I remember, being about 10 years old, when my parents told us that we were going on a family vacation, which we seldom did. I remember it being a hot summer. In the early '50s in July, we were going to the Catskill Mountains, better known as the Borscht Belt. We loaded up our Chevrolet for a five-day stay in a Catskill Bungalow Colony in Loch Sheldrake. Since we did not have reservations and every place was filled, we ended up in a cook-a-lane, a Yiddish word meaning "cooking alone." But it was really one big kitchen shared by many families that had ranges, ovens, and refrigerators. The bungalows had no kitchens. It was basically a communal kitchen that was supplied with pots and pans. Surely an inexpensive way to vacation for a large family.

We all piled into the car on Amboy Street, and guess what? The car engine did not turn over. My father always kept a set of jumper cables in the trunk, and within a few minutes, our trek started. It turned out to be a five-hour trip. We did get a flat on the way, and we stopped at the halfway mark (Red Apple Rest). There was no Quickway, so it was Route 17, the scenic route to the Jewish Alps. When stopping at Red Apple Rest, we would use the bathroom, and have some food, and within record time, five hours later we finally made it to Loch Sheldrake, A tremendous difference from Amboy Street. We were able to breathe fresh air and cool off in the country air. I even saw a real cow for the first time. My brothers and I would walk into the woods picking and eating blueberries. We would take along jars to collect fireflies, frogs, and salamanders. We never knew of sleep away camps like kids today. We even drank milk right from cows. We never knew about this way of life on Amboy Street. The only cow we saw was Elsie's picture on a milk bottle.

We stopped by some of the big resorts like Grossinger's, Kutsher's, Concord, Nevele, and the Browns. My father would tell the management we were thinking of coming back to stay for the summer the following year, even though we would never pay those prices. But they let us use the pool and facilities to see if we liked it. At night, we would again hit the big hotels to see a show. I recall going into the Pines and Grossinger's hotels to see popular comedians and singers who were performing there.

When we visited the smaller hotels like the Roxy in Kiamesha Lake, my brothers and I would perform in their talent shows. My brother Jack sang the song "Cry" just like Johnny Ray; he always received a standing ovation. We were always the best talent. You could see the pride in my parents' eyes.

The Borscht Belt was predominantly a Jewish American vacation resort that offered great entertainment and copious amounts of food. In its heyday, the region comprised over five hundred hotels and thousands of bungalow colonies. Today, the Borscht Belt is an eyesore. When airline flights became cheaper and more frequent, traveling to Florida and other destinations took over and thus began the demise of a beloved and beautiful era.

I was happy to have the experience of going to "the country," a world away from the streets of Brooklyn. But I also enjoyed going back to my friends on Amboy Street and back to playing in the streets. Who really cares about sleepaway camps, salamanders, frogs, and fireflies? I had more fun playing with my Spaldeen.

George Jessel in the Catskill Mountains

Tradition

Kids who grew up when I did are products of a Jewish culture derived from the depression. My parents were American born, but my grandparents were immigrants who came from Eastern Europe. My mom did speak some broken Yiddish, and there were many words I was able to pick up. We never kept a kosher home, but we never mixed meat with milk products. Some traditions we followed were going to Hebrew school and eating traditional food on the holidays, such as matzoh on Passover. My mom always made boiled chicken on Shabbat. She always made sure we all fasted on Yom Kippur. She also fasted even though she was allowed to eat because of her health. Ninety percent of our neighbors on Amboy Street were Jewish. Most of the schoolteachers were also predominantly Jewish. Nobody would drive their cars on the high holidays. Everyone watched one another, making sure they followed the holiday traditions. My mom would always tell me and my brothers to make sure we were noticed by the neighbors walking around the streets.

Amboy Street was starting to get Shabby

There are times when I close my eyes and visualize how Amboy Street looked. I lived in a row of about ten six-family multiple dwellings. To my right was one big building that was on the corner of Dumont Avenue, at 274 Amboy. Two of my friends lived in that building, Heshy Goldstein and Murray Kesden. On my left looking toward Blake Avenue were large tenement houses that contained at least twenty kids my age. Across the street were two-family homes, some with porches and others with a little garden that had a small area for planting. That was nice since there were no trees on our block. At each end of these dwellings were large apartment houses. Wherever you turned, there were kids playing on the streets.

Each of these large apartment houses had stores on the ground floor. I would say there were more than ten different types of stores including at least two candy stores and two grocery stores. As one can tell, you didn't have to travel far to shop. Over the years, these buildings started to decay. There wasn't a day where you wouldn't spot a mouse or a rat running across the street. If you turned a light on in the middle of the night, you would see cockroaches on the ceilings. I remember my mom telling me not to keep my hands off the bed when sleeping because I may get bitten. This was part of living in Brooklyn, where we bought mousetraps by the dozen. These were the conditions we lived under, and we accepted them for what they were.

I had one rich friend who lived in a two-family house across the street. His name was Sheldon Janowitz, and his family was in the home building business. I remember all my friends would sit in his Cadillac convertible for hours, never moving from the parking spot. It gave us the feeling of being rich, but I think we all would have rather played or talked about the Brooklyn Dodgers.

Larry Aaron

One of my brother Jack's best friends was Larry Aaron. He was a very good baseball player and was in a league at Betsy Head Park. The family lived directly across the street from us in a two-family house. His younger sister's name was Darling and she would always run out in the street naked. His mother's name was Blanche, and his father, Harry, was nicknamed Spider. He was a head shorter than his wife. He was an innovator and every month had a new invention.

I remember in the '50s, he came out with an idea to make bow ties that light up. He took it to a novelty shop, and they gave him an order. In today's world, one would make a call, and it would be produced in China in a short time. Since we had a large family living in our apartment, we were given the job to make those bowties. Larry's father brought all the pieces to our apartment to get it assembled with bulbs and batteries with the wires hidden in your pockets, and when there was contact, the bulbs would light up. It required some soldering and packaging that filled up our kitchen.

My whole family got to work and was paid by the pieces produced. Out of every ten produced, only four worked. It was a complete failure, and Spider lost his shirt, along with his bow ties.

Red Goldstein and his brother Heshy

Don "Red" Goldstein, a six-foot, six-inch center, was a great basketball player who played for Tilden High School. He played against Tony Jackson from Jefferson. He earned a scholarship to Louisville University, where he was an all-star. He was offered a professional scholarship but decided to go to dental school. He practiced dentistry in Westbury, Long Island., and lived in Melville, Long Island. He took care of my brother Bob's teeth. He was the first athlete that I knew from Amboy Street who became a celebrity. He was one of the greatest Jewish college players who came out of Brownsville.

Red played basketball with my brother Jack. They played in Mr. and Mrs. Persky's backyard on Amboy Street. They put up a basketball rim that was taken along with the backboard from my elementary school, PS 175. The older guys in the area would play on the mud because there was poor drainage. It was called Persky's Mud Garden. I did take some shots in the back of the house, but my brother Jack, who was three years older, played with his friends and started their own league. They lived right across the street from me in a two-family house at 253 Amboy Street. Moishe Persky, Howie Lesson, Morty Friedman, Jack Blumberg, Larry Aaron, and Don "Red" Goldstein were just a few of the guys I recall. They never made it to Madison Square Garden, but the Mud Garden sufficed.

Heshy who was Red's younger brother was a good friend of mine. They both had a difficult life. They lived a few buildings from me at 274

Amboy Street. It was difficult for Heshy. They were brought up by their grandmother we called Bubbe, a very sweet woman who spoke mostly Yiddish but knew a few English words. His father was deaf and dumb. I remember learning sign language and would communicate with him when meeting him on the street. I still know sign language, which I learned at five years old. My mom would invite both Heshy and his father over and give them lunch. Even though we barely made ends meet, my mom always had food in our house ready to give to anybody who needed it. Heshy went to the New York School of Printing, but shortly after he graduated, he worked for the U.S. Post Office. When he got married, he lived on Ocean Parkway in Brooklyn. Over the years, we lost contact and haven't spoken. It seems his wife gave him an ultimatum, saying if we marry I do not want you to have any relationship with your family and friends. It's hard to believe but he stopped speaking to his family and friends, it's sad but true.

I recall when I was about eight years old, Heshy and I would walk around the block with our pocket knifes. We would look for objects that were embedded in asphalt of the gutter, then we would dig them out. We found many coins and metal objects that we would hide in a dresser that was in an alleyway that led to the cellar of my building. I recall one day finding a two headed penny.

I would flip the coin and call heads, and I was always right. My friends couldn't believe my accuracy and I never told them.

Things I Remember

If someone found something in the street like a penny or a nickel and a friend noticed you picking it up, they would call halfies, and you had to share, fifty-fifty the value of that item.

We would have a ranking contest, which meant who could rank someone the lowest possible. I used to win by saying, "I'll rank you so low that you'll be sitting on the curb wiggling your legs." My friends would try to come out with a lower rank, but how much lower can you go?

Then there was the icees pushcart with different flavor syrups. The peddler of the cart would shave the ice with a metal contraption and put it in a paper cup. Then he would ask the customer which flavor they wanted, of which he would pour over the ice. That kept you cool on a hot summer's day.

We did lots of running around, playing games on our block. When it was time to rest, we would take a walk around the block or sit on the stoop.

When the temperature got really high and we needed to cool off, we would turn the fire hydrant on and shoot the water in the air. If a car came, they would roll up the windows and get a free carwash while driving down the street.

There were so many kids on Amboy Street that I pretty much only made friends with boys my age that lived on my end of the block.

There were back alleys that separated Herzl Street from Amboy. That was a place where there were crap games. It was hidden from the streets, and there were usually about six men who looked like gangsters playing craps. Somebody would always call the police. When the cops came to break up the game, they would run in different directions. They always took the money but would leave the dice. My friends would take the dice. I do remember a paddy wagon taking some of these gamblers back to the station. But in a few days, they were back in a different part of the alley. I am sure that Annie Hunk's boyfriend, Pacey, was part of this group.

I remember going to Morris Meat Store on Belmont Avenue. I recall my father getting some extra meat in the bag after giving the guy at the counter a tip.

Rimberg sold sporting goods, mostly league uniforms. I purchased my first baseball mitt at that store which I had to soak in oil for a week to get it soft. I would keep the ball in the glove making sure it have a good pocket.

All the houses were heated by black coal that would flow down a chute into the basement. Dark smoke from the chimneys would fill the skies. I loved to watch the coal slide down the chute when they raised the lever. The coal trucks would pick up the ashes. The janitors would load up the ash cans and roll them to the curb so the men could load them onto a truck. It went from the cellar and boilers to the refuse truck. The galvanized garbage cans were always dented.

I remember there were many false alarms because kids would pull the lever on the fire alarm box. These fire alarm boxes were situated on the corner every few blocks.

I remember men playing a violin or trumpet in the back alley, and people would wrap change in a tissue and throw it out of their windows as a tip for being serenaded.

I recall ordering seeds from school to plant in our flowerpots and having apples in the schools that were given away free. We had a fire drill almost every day. We would line up and get taken by the teachers a few blocks from the school. I had a shoeshine box where I walked around trying to earn some extra pennies.

There was the Fuller Brush man and the Electrolux vacuum cleaner salesmen going door to door.

At Ebbets Field, the Schaefer scoreboards lit up an *H* or the *E*, which told the fans if it was a hit or an error.

There were Kosher poultry stores where they cut off the head off from the chicken you ordered.

The sidewalk was divided into boxes, and because of the lines, games were made up every day. We sat on the curb near the gutter. If it was hot, we turned the "Johnny pumps" on to cool off. When a car passed, we would wash the car for free, making sure their windows were closed.

My Brooklyn, My Way

I remember the Bungalow Bar Truck coming down Amboy Street with the driver ringing its bells. All the kids would stop what they were doing, run to get money from their parents, and line up to order their ice cream. I loved the Mello-Rolls that were shaped like a cupcake. I also loved the Charlotte Russe. When we went to the candy store, we would order frappés and malteds, but when we ordered an egg cream, it was seltzer, milk, and syrup, never using any eggs or creams. If you ordered a coke, the syrup and seltzer were mixed by hand.

In my boyhood, I remember making a scooter from an old orange crate. I took the wheels off some old skates I found and nailed them to a board I found outside Feldman's lumberyard. I painted a number on the front, and I was ready to roll.

I also made a wooden zip gun that shot linoleum (oilcloth) pieces from a rubber band that was released by the flick of my thumb. There was a stone yard on Chester Street between Blake and Sutter Avenues wherein we would choose up sides and have a war. We would use the stones as a hiding place and then jump out and start shooting our guns. It was very scary place to play because it turned out to be a holding area for gravestones. We never went back.

Before I was born, Brownsville was a tough area. There were murders on its streets. My dad used to tell me about Murder Incorporated, better known as the Jewish Mafia, which was an organized crime group in the 1940s. He mentioned gangsters like Meyer Lansky, Dutch Schultz, Lucky Luciano, and Bugsy Siegel. When I was growing up, all I heard about those guys was that they hung out at the poolrooms. I was told they went around collecting money from people who played the numbers.

I remember a janitor who did the cleaning and maintenance at 274 Amboy Street, a large tenement building on the corner of Dumont. The building was separated by a row of houses by an alleyway. He was a nice Italian man who took his job very seriously. If a ball landed in the alley, we had to climb the fence to get the ball. He would sit in front, preventing any of my friends to enter his property to retrieve the ball.

We never knew his name, but we called him Talana. I think it originated by some old Jewish lady who only spoke Yiddish. Instead of saying Italian, she would say Talana. To get the ball that went over the fence, we would try to distract him. When he turned his head, we would lift a smaller player over the fence. He always carried a broom in his hand, and if he noticed we were on his property, he would chase us down the street and throw his broom at us.

Thank God we were faster than him!

Roger Elowitz and me are wearing plaid shirts can you find us? (1956)

Things we did as Kids that could have gotten us Killed

When reflecting on my early years, I am amazed how we experienced some of these activities without thinking twice!

* We drove in cars with no seat belts. We rode our bikes without helmets.
* There were kids who shot BB guns, which were air guns designed to shoot metallic ball projectiles called BBs. Kids would shoot at one another from rooftops, aiming at your back side.
* We played kick the Can and on many accessions hitting a friend in the head.
* We came down steep hills on a scooter with no brakes and no protection.
* We would swim at Betsy Head with no grown-ups as chaperones. There were two lifeguards talking to their girlfriends rather than protecting the thousands of people swimming in the pool.
* We would run behind a moving bus, and when it stopped, we would jump on the back. We would ride the bus until it stopped.
* We would fill up balloons with water and toss them from the roof, making a big splash when it hit the ground. Can you imagine if someone got hit with that balloon?
* Kids stayed out late; we never had a curfew. Nobody was around to watch us.

My Brooklyn, My Way

- Playing with firecrackers. We would light a cherry bomb, put it in an ash can, and then put the top back on, and when it went off, the lid would fly fifty feet in the air.
- There were times when we played Johnny on the Pony. The guy who stood in front was called the pillow. When a heavy guy would jump on the backs of my friends, it would cave in, and we all fell to the floor. Nobody got a broken back.
- I remember climbing a barbed wire fence and cutting my arm. I never told my mom and never got a tetanus shot. I wiped the blood and kept on climbing.

Can you believe we survived after noting just a few of the dangerous activities that were part of growing up in Brooklyn?

During the '50s, I remember our elementary school required the students to wear camphor balls around their necks to prevent polio before the vaccination was available. It seemed every two months, we had to take another vaccination.

Also in the '50s, the kids had to wear dog tags around their necks. It was made of polished steel, oblong in shape, with your name and blood type embossed in the metal. This would identify you if there was a nuclear missile attack.

They would have drills at school where they would sound a siren, and each pupil had to take cover under their desk. They made sure we were clear of the windows.

When I was twelve years old, I recall going on the parachute jump in Coney Island. When I was thirteen, I went with my friends to New York City to watch the ball drop on New Year's Eve. When I was fourteen years old, I went to downtown Brooklyn to the Paramount Theater to see Alan Freed hosting a rock and roll show. I was free to do just whatever I wanted. My parents never said be careful or come home early.

To get to Ebbets Field, we took the train, and when we got off, I remember stopping by a bowling alley on Empire Boulevard called Freddie Fitzsimmons. I went inside and noticed their alleys were not automated. They had pin boys putting the bowling pins on each dot in the lane and clearing the pins that fell. That was the first bowling alley I ever saw.

Sitting on the steps at Betsy Head Pool

Lundy's

There were times, mostly on special occasions like Mother's Day, my dad would take the family to Lundy's. It was, without a doubt, the best seafood restaurant in Brooklyn. Lundy's was on the corner of Emmons and Ocean Avenues in Sheepshead Bay.

I recall walking into this Spanish-style stucco building that seated more than 2,500 people at one time and served over 5,000 meals each day. It cost over $600,000 to construct, and that was a lot of money during the 1930s. It took up a full city block and looked more like a mansion than a restaurant. It was two stories high with two kitchens.

When you walked in to be seated, there was no maître d'. It is hard to believe it was up to the patrons to find a table. They had over two hundred African American employees serving the customers. I remember there were no tablecloths on the big wooden tables. A line would form down Emmons Avenue waiting to get in. Once you got in, you would walk around looking for parties getting up. You would stand around the table, and as soon as they paid the bill, you would sit right down. Sometimes, there were fights trying to sit down first. They had the best fish and lobster at reasonable prices. I remember starting out with clams on the half shell, which was in another room.

Lundy's lasted throughout the Great Depression and the war and closed down in 1979. Many years later, the family reopened a small portion of the restaurant. When I reminisce about going to Lundy's, I look back and feel fortunate to have eaten in this establishment during its heyday.

You could catch your own fish in Sheepshead
Bay or go across the street to Lundy's

Coney Island Joe's

Across the street from the BBC (Brownsville Boys Club) was a tiny frankfurter stand in a yellow and red cinderblock shack called (Coney Island Joe's.) it was located on Linden Boulevard and was owned by a school teacher. It became a regular stop where my friends and I would have a frank after playing ball at the BBC. The place was popular for their double hotdogs that was smothered with hot onions and red peppers. It opened in 1952 but today, it has been fenced in and shuttered. I remember when it was crowded with customers, and now it's very sad because it's crowded with a barbed wire fence that surrounds the building.

Family Business

Auto Barn Stores

    In the year 1957, my brother Herb, who is exactly ten years older than me, opened an auto parts store with his best friend, Mel Moskowitz who lived on Amboy street a few houses down the street. Mel joined the marines, and Herb went into the army. After serving their country, they both started working at a gas station on Powell Street. Herb went to Tilden, and Mel went to the New York School of Printing. They both took jobs from a Benny Cohen that owned Brownsville Auto Parts on East New York Avenue. Mel worked with sales, and my brother worked the counter.

    When they were in there mid twenties they opened their own auto parts store on Coney Island Avenue called H & M auto parts. There was much competition from stores like Jacoby, John Light, and Automotive Electric.

Because of their hard work and perseverance their business succeeded. In 1963, I joined the company, and within a few years we expanded and we opened in Lynbrook, Long Island and then expanded to Levittown and the stores we called Sunrise Auto Parts. When my younger brother Bruce got out of the army, he went to the Lynbrook location and I went to Levittown. I started an add campaign featuring " Mad Man Marty." We ran sales on auto parts with big discounts. Like crazy Eddie, they said I was insane.

At that time, 90 percent of all the calls we got were for American cars. The imports were mostly British, German, Italian, and some French. During those years, there were no Japanese cars in the USA. But as the years passed, the foreign market was starting to get popular. Herb saw the handwriting on the wall and opened up Globe Foreign Auto Parts. This was the first store to specialize in just foreign car parts in the New York area.

We expanded with more stores in Queens, Westchester, and Long Island and at one time we had a total of 19 stores. When Herb's son David graduated college, he joined our company. We went under the name of Auto Barn and still have locations in Long Island, N.Y. He was influential in setting up our popular website, autobarn.com, and he is currently the CEO. I am proud to say we have been in business for more than sixty years. My brother Herb, who started the business in 1957, still goes into work every day at the young age of eighty-eight.

I retired in 2012 at the age of seventy.

The Spaldeen and Stoopball

Mostly all my friends had a Spaldeen. We would go on the roof of the building, always finding a few that were lost in a stickball game. Yes, this high-bouncing pink tennis ball without the fuzz had hundreds of uses. We cut down a mop handle and used the stick for stickball, or we punched the Spaldeen, or we would play "Hit the Penny," or we just used our imagination. A good connection hitting the Spaldeen could send the ball two sewers. (That was the unit of measure at that time.) If the ball rolled into an open sewer, we would tape a clothes hanger to the end of the stick to scoop it up, or use the groceries claw poll.. I would boil the ball in my mom's chicken pot. That was a trick to make it bounce high and look new. And of course, I would clean the pot before Friday so my mother would make her soup. It was cheaper than spending fifteen cents for a new ball.

That spaldeen always came in handy when you wanted to play some kind of game with your friends. There was endless amount of games that were invented from one's imagination all from that little pink ball. One game that comes to mind was stoop ball. All you needed was a spaldeen and a stoop, and we had plenty of each along the streets of Brooklyn. Not only could you play with multiple players on each team, but you could also play "one on one." The game was played like baseball, usually a nine inning game. There were many different versions, like in certain parts of Brooklyn each hit would have a point value. When the first team reached 100 points, they would be victorious.

My Brooklyn, My Way

But, on Amboy street we played mostly nine innings and I preferred playing "one on one." Your opponent would stand in front of the stoop and throw the ball to different parts of the steps. The other player would play the outfield standings about fifteen feet back, facing the stoop. If he caught a ground ball or on a fly, that would be an "out." When there was three outs, you would change and reverse positions.

To get the most distance, the objective was to throw the ball against the point where the stair and riser meet. That would produce a line drive trajectory that accelerated and traveled a long distance. If the ball went over your opponents head landing on the other side of the street, that was considered a homer. A ground ball going past the fielder was a single. A line drive past your opponent was a double. and a ball just over the outfielder head was a triple. A game would take about a hour to play. In different neighborhoods there were optional rules like if the ball was hit off the stoop and took a funny bounce hitting a pebble causing the outfielder to misjudge and miss it, he would yell out "Hindu," and it would not count, that would be called a "do over."

A player could aim that ball to different parts of the stoop and could control where that ball would be hit. I remember there many times I would aim for the top step and the ball propelled across the street for a home run. The game "off the wall" was played the same way but instead of a stoop you would play against a building that had a molding ledge that when hitting the right spot would make the ball accelerate and take off to the other side of the street for a homer.

Stores in the Area

Pitkin Avenue had banks, movie theaters, and just about every type of store imaginable. There were many times we would take a five block stroll and walk to Pitkin Avenue, always looking in the windows but never buying any clothes. My knickers were in style for fifteen years, and who needed new? I was content just rolling down my cuffs.

There were two grocery stores on Amboy Street, and two candy stores each situated on both ends of the street. The one we used to frequent was owned by the Lipmans, corner of Amboy and Dumont. The candy store was owned by Sam Cohen directly across from Lipmans. We had a doctor's office and a lumber company called Feldmans. We had a laundromat, a Hebrew School run by Mr. Heifetz, Brill's barbershop, Shutzbank's drugstore, Ziggy's kosher delicatessen, a fruit store and even a sweet shop. I could throw my spaldeen to any of these stores from my apartment.

One of the most popular retail stores that I remember and shopped with my family was Fortunoff. The store was opened in 1922 by Max Fortunoff and his wife, Clara. It was under the El (train) on Livonia Avenue in East New York. Their first store specialized in housewares. It had a reputation of having a large selection of quality merchandise, great sales clerks, and low prices. It became a Brooklyn landmark. At one time, they had eight different shops specializing in different household items along with jewelry all located under the elevated subway in "LA" - Livonia Avenue. There was one store I remember going into with my father that was for returns and defective merchandise only.

The neighborhood started to change, and that part of Brooklyn that I always passed when going to Thomas Jefferson High became one of the poorest neighborhoods. Fortunoff then moved out to Westbury, Long

Island, and sadly, after many years of being in business and not being profitable, the Fortunoff and the Mayrock families sold their major interest in their business.

I remember Sol's ice cream parlor on New Lots Avenue, where my father took the family for ice cream treats. Sol's had the best frappés, but our favorite was called "Tall in the Saddle." There was enough ice cream, slices of banana, crushed fruits, and nuts to supply an army or even Francis, our back neighbor. We would all sit around the table, each putting our spoons in one at a time; today, we call that double-dipping. But who really cared?

Another popular place was Jahn's ice cream parlor that served "The Kitchen Sink." It was an outrageous amount of ice cream, even for my family. But we preferred Sol's over Jahn's.

Holidays

If you walked through the alleyways of Amboy Street five days after the high holiday of Yom Kippur, you would notice a phenomenon and a definite memorable sight before your eyes. There were sukkahs in the back of most tenements. As a young boy about six years old, I had no idea what these little buildings were. They symbolize the temporary dwellings that were built by Jews during the time of the Exodus, when the Jewish people left Egypt. It refers to the shelters that protected our ancestors during the night and shielded them from the hot sun during the day. It describes how the Israelis lived and built these temporary dwellings in the Sinai desert for forty years. These shelters protected our ancestors on their way out of Egypt on their journey toward freedom.

This remarkable custom is still done today. These structures are made with plant material such as palm leaves, branches, and wood. It was a room erected by the tenants in my building to pray and celebrate this holiday for a period of seven days. I remember the decorations with different fruits hanging from the ceiling with a table and chairs to sit on. The people from our building would come down to eat their meals. I recall dipping the challah in honey.

As a young boy, I was asked to help build this sukkah in the back of my building. I recall throwing branches on the roof of the sukkah. I remember eating, singing, and listening to the older people pray and tell stories about the scriptures and the significance of the holiday. It showed me that people could survive without material possessions. It is a happy holiday that demonstrates that you can be content with just the essential things in life. But most of all, I was a young boy who was proud to help build a sukkah.

I also remember on Passover, all the kids would go outside with a big bag of nuts. We would play games like rolling the nuts against a wall. You had to roll it to the wall and hit the other nuts. Many times, there were about fifty nuts on the sidewalk. I remember winning so many nuts that I needed the help of my friends to help me bring them home. After eating most, I think it got me a little nuts.

School

Life was very easy. One reason was I was never pressured to do well in school. I think in my childhood years my parents thought more about working and having food at our table. I am sure they wanted us to do well but left it to us. Nobody ever checked my homework. When I received my report card, I would hand it to my mom to sign. She never even noticed my grades. I would point to the spot to sign, which she did, and I handed it back to my teacher. My parents never stressed how important college was; getting a good job seemed more important to them at that time. But somehow we knew what was right and all my brothers either graduated or attended college. I was not a serious student until my senior year in high school. I attended night school at Brooklyn college for six years, while working during the day.

When I was five, I went to Public School 175, which was a few blocks from where I lived. I remember my kindergarten teacher, Mrs. Porback. All through the sixth grade, I had great teachers like Mrs. Riggons, Mrs. Sirota, Mrs. Stein, Mrs. Rubin, and a Mr. Gardener, who would teach sex education, even though he was a social studies teacher. I was so proud in the fifth grade when Mrs. Stein made me a crossing guard. That job came with a sash and a badge. I remember making sure the pupils were not standing in the gutter until the light turned green.

When I attended public school, every student was required to visit the dentist to have their teeth examined. After the dentist finished their work, they would have to sign a completion slip and return it to the school. We used a dentist named Dr. Simmons. For some undetermined reason, he only gave my family temporary fillings, but we always got our completion slip. But within a year, the fillings would fall out, and we had to start all over.

My Brooklyn, My Way

In my second year at public school, my teacher's name was Mrs. Dubin, and her twin sister also taught there. You were not able to tell them apart, but they were both ugly redheads. I recall the assistant principal. Her name was Ms. Lena Cherichetti, whom everyone feared. Every morning, you would see her wearing a white-and-black polka-dotted dress, her hair pulled back in a bun, and her cowbell in her right hand, which she'd ring in the schoolyard. We had to line up in a straight line on Hopkinson Avenue before the start of school. Nobody was ever late, but if you were, she would tap your shoulder to see her in her office. She always wore the same dress. That may be the reason why she was a spinster, but she did have the largest collection of antique dolls, if that means anything.

I recall doing my homework in the street with my friend Michael Charney. One day, my fountain pen started to leak. I filled it with green ink that spilled all over my paper. I don't know why, but I handed it in, having green blotches all over the paper, it was unreadable. The teacher gave me a red *F* written across the paper with explicit instructions that my mom had to sign the paper. When I showed it to her, she never questioned the *F*. She thought it was a nice colorful Christmas design I drew with red and green ink, and signed it.

I started my junior high school years at PS 66 at an all-boys school called Lewis Wallace Junior High that went through ninth grade. It was a very tough school. I remember witnessing many fights after school. The girls went to PS 84, also in walking distance from Amboy Street.

When walking to PS 66, we had to cross Rockaway Avenue and go through a low-rental project. There was a metal chain link that separated the grass from the walkway. Black kids would run down that sidewalk and push you over the fence. They called it "Over the Green Trolley." If you said anything, they would say, "You mess with me, you'll mess with the Gaylords." We just picked up our books and walked away.

On your first day at school, the older students would sing to you the words from my alma mater song. It went like this:

> "We welcome you to Wallace High. We're mighty glad you're here. We'll set the air, reverberating with a mighty cheer. We'll sing you in, we'll sing you out, we'll make you have a mighty shout. Hail, hail, the rookies are here, and we welcome you to Wallace High."

My Brooklyn, My Way

    The freshman were then punched and kicked by the seniors after the song. That was your initiation for entering PS 66, one of the toughest schools in Brooklyn. I recall on Wednesday's we had assembly and our dress code was a shirt and tie.

    Mr. Tobias was my woodworking teacher who would hit you with a yardstick if you were misbehaving. He would stress that you tuck your tie in the top button of your shirt. This was his safety device making sure your tie did not get stuck in the cutting machine, which could pull your head into the saw and get it chopped off. A very ingenious safety device. When he was not looking, the students would be making oilcloth guns, making sure they were sanded and painted. He never said a word as long as your tie was tucked in your shirt.

    PS 66 had an indoor swimming pool. We all went swimming naked. The teacher, Mr. Esposito, also walked around naked. I never understood why we didn't wear bathing suits because it looked like a nudist colony. There were many kids who never came out of the water. Sorry, but we never did take a class picture.

    In my senior year at PS 66, a new school was built PS 263, that was a half mile from one another. I was part of the first graduating class. I remember having the students help move all the supplies to the new location. We would walk from one school to another, carrying supplies in the street to PS 263. I think I missed two weeks of school walking instead of learning. They could never get away with that today.

    I remember two very good teachers named Mr. Peck and Mr. Dembo. They both worked at the HES (the Hebrew Educational Society). Mr. Peck lived across the street from me on Amboy Street. He taught math. Adolph Dembo, a science teacher, was a strong liberal and the first person I knew who broke the color barrier and married a black woman. His first wife, named Dorothy, passed away at a young age, and he remarried a black woman and later in years lived in Oceanside, Long Island, New York.

    He was a mentor to many students. He was influential in helping students develop their careers. He even coached many teachers to become principals in schools throughout Brooklyn, and a few became district superintendents. He was well respected and helped many families that had both financial as well as social problems.

    Since I moved to Canarsie, my high school was Thomas Jefferson. If I stayed in Brownsville, I would have attended Tilden. Jefferson was a great school that always had great basketball and football teams. I played second trumpet for the marching band and was also in the orchestra. It was great meeting new friends who lived in East New York. Before that, most of my friends lived on Amboy Street. Jefferson had some of the best teachers in the city, many taking prominent jobs in the educational field.

One teacher I recall taught us how to use the typewriter. His name was Mr. Rappaport. He was a slight old man who loved to teach typing, even though it was the most boring subject. I always thought when he went to sleep at night, he would count letters rather than sheep. He would use a microphone and keep on repeating letters over and over. We all had Underwood typewriters in front of us, and we had to type the letter he would call out, always keeping eight fingers on the keys. I never learned where the letters were but always used one finger. This class helped many girls become secretaries which was a popular profession in the 50's and 60's.

Mr. Rappaport wore the same woolen suit every day, even if it was a hot day. The reason why I know it was the same suit is there were students that would spit on the back of his jacket when he passed by. When you saw him weeks later, you could still notice the stains on his jacket. One day, my friends and I planned to all hum at the same time. This was our way of getting even with him for always yelling out those letters. This drove him crazy. He'd run around the class thinking his microphone had static until he realized it was a joke. He never smiled but continued to call out those letters.

Ms. Cherichetti displays her doll collection (1947)

The Lone Ranger

On rainy days, I would watch cowboy movies on TV. My hero was the Lone Ranger and his Indian companion, Tonto. I always thought that the Lone Ranger took advantage of Tonto. He had him do all the dirty work. He would sit back and give Tonto orders like make him disguise himself by taking on a different identity that could have gotten him killed. I remember one episode where he told Tonto to disguise himself as a tumbleweed, go into town, and see what he can pick up. Tonto had to roll into town and bring back information. I have no idea what the Lone Ranger was doing, probably polishing his silver bullets.

But he was my hero because with his silver bullets, he never shot to kill the enemy. It may be because silver was expensive, and he didn't want to waste a bullet. He would always disappear in the horizon, never saying good-bye; but in a cloud of dust, he would yell, "Hi-Yo, Silver, Away!" and gallop away with the speed of light into the sunset, with the dust flying in Tonto's face. I think Tonto thought he was crazy because he would leave behind an expensive silver bullet, and then the people in town would ask, "Who was that masked man?" And a little old lady would say that was the Lone Ranger, never giving Tonto any credit, even though he did all the dirty work.

Horn & Hardart

I forgot how I got there, but I remember eating at the automat. I would presume my dad drove me there because I know there were none in my immediate area. It was considered the first American fast-food chain, the Horn & Hardart. You would walk into this restaurant, and against the wall, there were rows of chrome and glass cabinets that were coin-operated. If you found something you wanted to order, you would insert your nickels and pull a lever, and a door would open. There were many types of sandwiches, soups, or a variety of hot meals and even a slice of apple pie. There were no waiters, no tips, and no cash registers. You brought your dish to the table and ate your food. They did have someone working behind the machines, filling them up. There was also a change booth where you could get your nickels. Since we didn't have to tip waiters, my family was only too happy to take our food on our own. I think that is one reason for the success of Horn & Hardart. I remember the woman in the glass-enclosed booth who had a dispenser in front of her that stamped out nickels to make change.

There is a joke about a drunk who strolled into the Horn & Hardart and put two nickels in the dispenser, and when he opened the door, a sandwich came out. He tried it again, and the same thing happened. He then pulled a chair in front of the dispenser, and each time, food appeared. The manager walked over to him and told him he must move because he was blocking the aisle. The drunk got loud and curt and started screaming, "I finally found a slot machine that pays off, and you're chasing me away!"

Music

Music in the '50s was entirely different from what it is today. Every day, it seemed a new rock and roll record would be cut, and a new Brooklyn singing group would be discovered. Many groups from Brooklyn appeared on the top of the charts. Most of these groups were one-song wonders. But we loved the music, and my friends and I would also sing these songs. It was not unusual to hear these groups while walking around the area. That's where they practiced, on the corner, singing, making up their own lyrics and melodies as they went along. They would harmonize until the song was perfect. These were the songs we grew up to in the '50s. This was the music we played and danced to constantly. These were the songs that made us fall in love. I remember going to the Brooklyn Paramount where they would have about ten groups appearing on stage. These were the oldies but goodies that will never die.

But please don't ask me about today's music. I don't remember lyrics to any songs or recognize any groups. I do not know the difference between Lady Gaga and Lady MacBeth, except Lady MacBeth had a better voice. But if you ask me about the Everly Brothers' "Wake Up Little Susie" or Fats Domino's "Blueberry Hill," I would know every word from those songs. I used to sing them constantly. That was part of what Brooklyn really was. The lyrics explained to me that there was more to life than playing ball in the streets. There was something else called girls. I realized at that time that making out with a girl was better than connecting with that Spaldeen.

I remember hearing my older brothers saying they went on a date to Plum Beach to watch the submarine races. I was old enough to understand that there were no submarines in Brooklyn. And, besides that, how could you watch a race underwater? Things were starting to click in my mind and I realized that besides sports, there was something else and that was girls.

S&H Stamps or was it King Korn Stamps?

Looking back when I was a kid, I think about my dad and how shrewd he was. He was also frugal and was always a step ahead, always getting his money's worth. I remember a funny story when a supermarket was giving away an extra two hundred King Korn stamps with any purchase. My dad took his car and told my mom and brothers to get into the car because we were going to a supermarket. He said today was grand opening day, and not only were they giving away two hundred stamps with any purchase but they were also giving out triple King Korn stamps. Since it was one purchase per customer, he made sure we took along extra jackets. He would send us all in, making many trips, making sure we would disguise ourselves wearing different jackets. I recall buying one apple or a few grapes just to make a purchase so I could get the bonus stamps. My father accumulated so many stamps that we were able to get a free tape recorder. At night we would all sit around the tape recorder singing songs. I still have the tape of my mom singing "My Yiddishe Mama."

Another hobby my father had was taking out bank accounts. He had at least twenty-five bank accounts with an average balance of ten dollars in each bank. Every time a branch was opened, he would receive gifts for opening a new account, he was always first in line.

Family Values

I feel that the world today would be a much better place if people had lived and experienced how life was during the fifties. Some people may look back and say they were tough years, but our parents taught us to show respect and to study and that by working hard, you will succeed. And especially, we were shown that there is more to life than material things.

Brownsville was a special place to live. I cherish all my memories, and without any doubt, these were some of the best years of my life. Without making any changes, I would live my childhood days all over again. I understand that throughout Brooklyn, there are neighborhoods with their own individual charm. When Brooklynites think of their upbringing, it brings smiles to their faces. There were always many kids who were ready to play any type of game. The streets were safe, and our parents thought nothing that we stayed out late.

I'm sure when you visualize your block, there were probably many stores to shop. Amboy had about ten stores without ever crossing a street. Whatever you wanted to do was a short walk away. We were fortunate to live within walking distance to Pitkin Avenue, which was the main shopping area in Brownsville.

I still have unforgettable memories of my childhood days. I may forget current things, like what I had for dinner the other night, but I still remember the good old days.

There was always a Blumberg

It seemed like everyone knew the Blumberg boys. Because there were five boys living in one apartment, we covered every age group. Since we were about three years apart in age, just about every kid on Amboy Street was friends with one of us. We all loved sports and excelled in the games we played. If anyone on the block needed an extra player, they would always find a Blumberg who could fill that spot.

My parents would never tell my brothers that they could not participate in some sort of game. My mom would never say, "Sorry, my son Marty has to study," or "He has to finish his homework." She never showed favoritism toward any one child, but whenever she was alone with one of us, she would say, "You are the best."

Amboy Street was safe, and parents did not think twice about letting their kids play from dawn till dusk. We always finished our games even if there was not enough light. We would play under the lamppost or in the dark. It seemed like that Spaldeen was always visible. It appeared to light up bright pink at night.

My brothers and I had limited toys. The next best thing was to use our imagination. We kept busy by inventing games and playing in our apartment.

Toys

Growing up in my boyhood, I had only four toys - a toy guitar, a cowboy gun, a Howdy Doody puppet, and a Spaldeen. Even today, I still own a Howdy Doody puppet that I use to entertain my grandchildren,

On Amboy street, we had a large collection of 78 rpm records that we played on our Victrola. My older brother Herb liked to listen to parody songs from Yiddish singers like Mickey Katz. He would often sing along to "Levkowitz the Cop." He knew every word. A few songs that I heard constantly were "Duvid Crockett, King of Delancey Street," and "Levkowitz the Cop," the lyrics were:

> "I'm Levkowitz the Cop. When I blow my whistle the cars they better stop, and if they don't stop I'll give a knock. I'm Levkowitz the Cop."

Shoemaker

The year was 1953. I was twelve, and my friends and I were playing many different games. The sidewalks were divided into five-foot-by-five-foot squares. These cracks in the pavement made it very easy to make up games with our Spaldeen. We played "Hit the Penny" using two squares, "Box Ball," and "Closest Penny to the Line." We never ran out of games to play.

But there was one game just about everyone forgot about, and that was called "packs," or some called it "Heels." A pack is the heel from a shoe. Kids would walk the streets with four or five packs in their pockets in case someone challenged them to a game. I was always ready! Sometimes, you lost to any player if they landed on your pack. If that happened, you had to give it up to the other player. I lost one of my packs to my friend, which was a fat heel called a fat pack, after he landed on it.

I now needed a new pack to play on the street. I already had a slider that could knock my opponent off the line. I had a sticker heel that when I threw it, there was no bounce, so it stuck to the spot it landed. What I needed was a high heel that was just about impossible for another pack to land on.

So I went to Mr. Green, who owned the shoe repair shop on Amboy Street. When I spoke to him, I found him amazing. He was able to talk to me while repairing shoes with a mouthful of nails that he stored in his mouth by size. We had a complete conversation, and at the same time, he would spit out each nail as he did his work. Amazingly, he never swallowed any of the nails. I purchased a thick new heel for five cents.

This game of (heels) packs was played on the street by throwing your pack to the cracks on the sidewalks. You would take turns trying to get to the third crack in the sidewalk. The closest to the line would be the winner.

My Brooklyn, My Way

So you see, to be a champ at packs, you had to have three or four different heels to change during a game. Thanks to Mr. Green, I became the champ in heels.

    Mr. Green had another job, and that was painting your name on the back of your Levi's jacket. It took a day to dry, but he would paint your jacket with flames in chartreuse and bright colors. It looked very cool walking down the street with your name painted with lightning background. Then there were the "hard guys" who painted their names on their black leather jackets. I always wondered, while Mr. Green painted these jackets, if he took the nails out of his mouth or if he replaced them with different-colored paintbrushes.

Movies

When I went to the movies, my mom would pack my lunch in a brown paper bag, give me an extra twenty-five cents for candies and a drink, and tell me to pick out a nice dish the movie theater gave away as an extra. We never needed a chaperone; we all felt safe. Since I lived on Amboy Street, we only had to walk four blocks to the theater, right past Betsy Head Pool. After paying the twenty-five-cent admission, you would think you were entering a delicatessen. It seemed that most kids had a deli sandwich in their bag. I always ended up by the candy counter, buying a box of candies for a nickel. I remember sitting in the movies for five hours watching about fifteen cartoons, two cowboy movies, a newsreel, a feature film, and two serials. A serial was a continuation of the prior week's film.

Usually, if it was a rainy Saturday, I would go with my friends to the movie theaters that were walking distance from Amboy Street. There were two movie theaters that I went to that were diagonally across the street from each other, the People's Cinema and the Ambassador Theater located on Saratoga and Livonia Avenues. They were both located under the IRT train, so when a train passed, you could hear the noise. I always questioned why they would build two theaters across from each other under a train.

We even had 3-D movies, where you would be given a pair of cardboard glasses. On the way to the movies, we would stop at the pickle store, and with two cents, you could buy a pickle on Livonia Avenue by putting your dirty hands in a barrel, trying to find the largest sour pickle. When you walked into the movie theater you could not help to smell those sour pickles.

You could not help to hear the noise from the trains while watching a movie. But after a few shows, you got used to it, and it just seemed like sound effects. Sometimes it was so crowded that I remember sitting on the stage watching the movie lying down. I remember the older kids would sneak in. The way they did it was one kid would pay and then open the emergency side door, and ten of his friends would sneak in free. Once they were inside, they would spread out, and the matrons would look for them. It was very disturbing because those matrons looking for those kids pointed their flashlights at your face while they searched. They were never able to find them in the dark.

The theater, besides the smell of pickles, smelled like spoiled cold cuts and was a real dump. One time when I was eating my popcorn, I noticed a mouse sitting next to me eating my popcorn. When I tried to scare it away, it ran down the seat and got stuck on the floor from all the dried-up soda. As a treat, I would buy bonbons, which were balls of ice cream covered with chocolate. I remember I always made sure to get that free piece of dinnerware my mom asked me for. My mom's dishes consisted of the complete set.

The People's Cinema Movie Theatre

Choir

I had to be about eleven years old playing on Amboy Street in Brownsville. A man walked up to me and started a conversation. He asked me if I was interested in singing in his choir for the high holidays. He said he would pay me ninety dollars, and he asked me to invite any other friends who may be interested. That was a lot of money, and I told him I would ask them. Two of my friends, Mike Charney and David Friedman, all agreed. I don't remember if I even asked my parents.

He came around the next day, and we told him it was something we would entertain. He told us that we would rehearse once a week, and he would give us some pocket change sometimes as much as a quarter after each practice. I told him we all couldn't read a word of Hebrew, but Mr. Pfizer said he would teach us.

Believe it or not, Mr. Pfizer drove a Kaiser. He would pick us up and drive us to a temple on Pitkin Avenue to practice. There were about three older grown-ups in our group. Mr. Pfizer, our leader, had a tuning fork to start the lesson. We practiced and practiced and memorized the hymns. We were ready to visit temples to audition to be hired to sing for the high holidays.

Now, since Mr. Pfizer had a Kaiser and after the holidays paid us ninety dollars, you cannot call him a miser. We were hired by an Orthodox temple near Prospect Park called Temple Isaac. Since it was during Rosh Hashanah and Yom Kippur, we had to sleep over in the home of one of the members of the congregation since we were not allowed to ride on the holidays. Mr. Pfizer would park his Kaiser ten blocks away so nobody would see him drive home. I remember each solo I sang, and I know every word even today.

My mom and dad came to the services and listened to me sing. Tears came to my mom's eyes as she listened to her son Motchkee chant in an Orthodox temple, never ever having a Hebrew lesson. As a young child, all I ever did was get out of my knickers, get dressed with my pants without holes, and walk around the streets with my friends, never entering a synagogue. By the way, Mr. Pfizer paid me the ninety dollars, which I gave right to my mom. I then sang three more years with an increase in salary each year. I was making over $150 for singing in the choir. My main solo was a prayer called "Habain, Habain," which I could chant every word from this prayer even today. I still can't read a word of Hebrew, but because of Mr. Pfizer, I became a little wiser.

Hebrew School

Mostly all my friends who lived on Amboy Street attended a Hebrew school. The school they went to was run by Mr. Heifetz and his wife, Molly. The Hebrew school was on Blake and Herzl and was conducted in their storefront schoolroom. There were two rooms in this so-called religious school. Mr. Heifetz taught in the front room, and his wife, Molly, would teach the beginners in the back room.

Mr. Morris Heifetz was not very tall, but he was tough. There were many fights in his class. He would chase after you in the schoolroom, one hand holding his yarmulke so it wouldn't fall and the other hand swinging his ruler. He took teaching very seriously, and if you were fooling around in his classroom, it was his nature to pull you out of your seat and push you around. He would scream so loud that his wife would run out from the back room telling him to quiet down. Rabbi Heifetz's main focus was to prepare the boys to learn, read Hebrew, and chant from the Torah for their bar mitzvah.

His wife would teach the boys (never saw a girl) the symbolic letters and how to read Hebrew. Nobody ever knew the meaning of the words they were reading. After we learned the letters and symbols, we would be promoted to the front room, where Rabbi Heifetz would walk up and down the aisle listening to each boy's pronunciations.

My problem was my parents never enrolled me in a Hebrew school, and I was approaching my thirteenth birthday. They finally decided to speak to Mr. Heifetz, and he was able to give me a crash course, and I memorized the blessing "Barukh atah adonai, eloheinu melekh ha 'olam." In less than two months, I was in the synagogue on Amboy street near Sutter Avenue, chanting the Jewish blessings and had my Bar Mitzvah . It was held early in the morning, and my youngest brother Bruce overslept and missed the service. But thanks to Mr. and Mrs. Heifetz I became a man.

Barbershop

What a great idea for a barbershop in today's world. While you are taking a haircut, you get serenaded. On the corner of Amboy Street and Blake Avenue in Brownsville, Brooklyn, there was a small barbershop with three chairs. It was owned by the Brill brothers, who looked like identical twins in their '90s. But being about nine years old at the time, they were probably in their fifties. Everyone seemed old to me, but now it's the reverse—everyone seems young.

When I walked to the public school, I would pass this barbershop, always looking in the storefront window, smiling to the Brill brothers. I think they were immigrants from Romania. They both had very thick accents and had long messy hair. I think they both needed haircuts. When I looked through the window, I would notice customers taking haircuts and others taking a shave. They would use a long-edge razor blade, always sharpening it with a leather strap that was hanging from the chair. There were always customers waiting in the seats that were lined up against the window.

I remember my parents taking me and my brothers to a barbershop on Hopkinson Avenue near Livonia. The owner's name was Mr. Turchin, and for about fifty cents, my father would tell him to give me a trim, which was much less money than a full haircut.

One day, I persuaded my parents to take me for a haircut to the Brill brothers. Since it was on the same block that I lived, I went there for a haircut. I got there at noon, and I was finished by 3:00 p.m. I waited a half hour until I was told to have a seat. They stopped what they were doing to have their lunch. They cooked in the back, and when the food was ready, they sat down to have their meal. After lunch, they both took out their violins and started to serenade their customers for an hour. They played rhapsodies by Bach and Tchaikovsky in unison. They were very good.

When I got home, my mom said they did not cut your hair short enough. I told her, "I don't care. I feel very sophisticated, and now I will let my hair grow long like Ludwig van Beethoven." She had no idea what I was talking about.

There was a barbershop on almost every Brooklyn Street

First TV Set

We were the first in our neighborhood to buy a TV set. It was a black and white, seven-inch View Tone that was always breaking down. My dad kept extra tubes and was always fixing the set. I remember one tube, the 6NF7, that was always going bad. One day, my dad brought home a large magnifying glass that he attached on the picture tube, and then a few weeks later, he attached a reddish-tinted plastic that stuck to the glass. This made our small black and white TV set change into a large color TV set.

Many of our neighbors would visit us, bringing in chairs to watch some shows like *The Ed Sullivan Show, The Milton Berle Show,* and even Joe Louis when he fought for the boxing championship. We always had people in our apartment. There were times when I would watch cowboy films with my brothers like *Roy Rogers, Gene Autry,* and *The Lone Ranger.* I also watched *Howdy Doody,* and even today, I still have the puppet.

Our TV always had interference. It would take about five minutes before the set warmed up and a picture came on. There were times when there weren't any programs on, and we would sit by the TV looking at a pattern until a show came on. To get the picture clear was a very difficult job. We had a roof antenna that when we would open the window, my dad would go on the roof to move it in different directions to get the TV clear. I remember yelling to the roof, "Good," "Worse," or "Better," and finally when it was clearer, my dad would come down from the roof. Ten minutes later, the wind would blow, and the TV's reception became worse. We had an indoor antenna we called rabbit ears that never really helped that much. We were constantly moving it around.

At night, I would open up the sofa, and we would all find spots on the convertible to watch TV together. My dad would go to into his room early so he could get a good night's sleep so he could deliver the mail. I remember one evening, my elder brother Herb would come home from a date, and he loved to watch Steve Allen play the piano. He would yell, "I am coming in for a landing." We would all reposition ourselves on the bed to make room for him. But this time, the leg caved in, and the bed collapsed to the floor. After that, I had a new job, and that was to pile books under the broken leg so the bed was level.

It's hard to forget those early years and the fun we had as a family. Today, I say to myself that when I was younger and we only had three channels to choose from, there was always something to watch. Today, I have over two hundred channels and can't find a good show.

The old days are gone, and I am sorry to say they are not coming back. I look at the kids of today, and all I see is their cell phones attached to their heads. When I go to the theater, restaurants, even while crossing a busy main intersection, they are always on their phones texting or talking. The only stimulation these kids are getting is in their fingers. These cell phones have stopped them from all physical activities. As a boy from Brooklyn, I was more active in one day than they are in a month.

Today, if a kid loses their phone, they tell their parents, and they spend a few hundred dollars for a new smartphone. We never had a smartphone; in fact, we never even had a dumb phone. Something is not right; these kids of today are not running or playing together. They do not know what fun and exercise are really about. If only those good old days could come back, instead of a kid having a phone in their back pocket, they would have a Spaldeen.

7 inch View Tone TV

These Were Some of the Games I Played in the Streets

It seems the games I played with my friends as a young boy required a very small or no investment.

Ringolevio was fun. It was made up of two teams. One team would close their eyes and count to ten. The other team would run around and hide. The idea was to touch a person and say, "Caught, caught ringolevio, one, two, three." That would send him to jail. One member on your team was a jailer, trying to prevent the captured from being freed.

Punchball was also like baseball. The pitcher on the opposite team would pitch the ball on a bounce to you. When hit, you would run to first base. If you did not have enough men, you would not play with a pitcher. You would throw the ball up like serving in tennis. It was called Fongo. You would make a fist and punch the Spaldeen and then run to first base.

We played Kick the Can in the streets, mostly on the corner where we were able to use the sewers as bases. It was played like baseball without a ball. You would kick the can and run to first base.

"Pickup" was a game played with a ball. Your partner would throw the Spaldeen high in the area, and your opponent would try to catch it on a short hop which was six inches off the ground.

I remember a person named Irving Blitz who would stand at half court and make one shot after another on the basketball court. He also coached many basketball teams to championships.

My Brooklyn, My Way

We played a game called "Off the Wall." The idea was to hit a bump along a building. The ball would take off, and if it went on the sidewalk across the street, that was a home run.

Hit the Penny was played on the sidewalk. A penny or a popsicle stick was placed on the crack of the box on the sidewalk crack. You would stand opposite each other, and it was played with two and sometimes four friends. You scored when you hit the penny.

Hide-and-seek was played with one guy closing his eyes with his head on a pole, counting to ten and then trying to find where your friends were hiding. It took long unless you made up boundaries.

My other game I loved was tops. You would wind your top with a string and throw it in the gutter, trying to hit your friend's top and split it in half while it was spinning. Some of these tops had such sharp points that when thrown down hard, you could do damage to your friend's top if you hit its soft spot. When that happened your opponents top was in two pieces.

Games Girls Played

The girls would always be playing jump rope. The girls also used the Spaldeen to play "A, my name is Alice." On every initial going up the alphabet, they would cross their legs over the bouncing ball. The girls who were more advanced would do double Dutch. Many boys who passed by would ask to jump in, but they would misstep on their first try. It took a lot of practice and conditioning and hand-eye coordination. Double Dutch involves two rope turns, a jump rope, and a jumper in the middle. It seemed very difficult because of two ropes moving in opposite directions, and the jumper had to keep on jumping till it got twisted, and you couldn't turn the rope anymore. Hopscotch was also a popular game.

Baseball

During my early years when I was about twelve years old, a popular thing to do was collect baseball cards. You would buy about five baseball cards with a piece of gum for five cents a pack produced by Topps. Kids would walk around with two stacks in their hands; one pile was their good cards that they didn't play with, and the other pile was to trade or flip. There were kids who had so many cards they would store them in shoeboxes. You never knew what you would get in a pack of cards, and every kid wanted the Brooklyn Dodgers players.

Flipping cards was an art. There were kids who could flip fifty heads in a row. You would flip the card to the ground, making about ten revolutions until it hit the ground. The idea was to match what your opponent threw first and match heads (picture) or tails (player biographies). The picture of the players was heads, and the statistics on the back was tails.

Another game we played with the cards was tossing them against the wall. The idea was to throw what we called a leaner. The card would lean against the wall, and you would try to knock it down. The person with the most leaners would win all the baseball cards thrown, sometimes fifty cards. If there were no leaners, the closest card to the wall was the winner. Many arguments broke out trying to measure the closest card.

When they first came out kids only wanted the gum. But, it all changed when the cards were more important then the gum. They went from being largely a premium intended to help drive sales of candy and gum to a standalone product. Players like Mantle, Clemente, Aaron, Mays, and Koufax are just a few of the baseball players to have rookie cards in the early 1950s. These cards had smaller production, so they were hard to get and became collectibles to the hobby enthusiasts.

I happen to like Bazooka gum the best. They made the biggest bubbles, and the flavor lasted the longest.

Topps

The Topps company started to produce a baseball card to compete against the Bowman company. They enclosed five cards with a piece of gum that sold for five cents a pack. Sid Berger was hired in 1951 to design a card with baseball players, along with a piece of gum. It became very popular with every kid saving their best players.

In 1952, Topps produced their first series, and it took off all around the country. The business was started on the kitchen table in his apartment on Alabama Avenue in Brooklyn. In 1952, the first modern baseball card set was released in two series: a low-number (1–310) and a high-number (311–407) product. The first series sold out very fast, in fact, too fast. When they ordered the second series, their expectations were too high, and with kids going back to school, the second series tanked and did not sell. Their timing and ordering was poor, and the cards sat in crates and were dead inventory.

Since they needed the space for the 1953 cards to arrive, they decided to load up their trucks and dump the pallets in the Atlantic Ocean. Today, we call it polluting the ocean. They decided to take a tax write-off, but if they kept those cards that were all in mint condition, it would have been worth millions of dollars in today's market. In retrospect, I don't think that was a great business decision. The Mantle rookie cards and Jackie Robinsons were in these unsold cases and in today's market would be valued in the millions.

Poem

Moshe at the Bat

by Martin Lewis Blumberg

The outlook wasn't brilliant in Brooklyn one fine day.
There was a big stickball game going on in the gutter, not the alleyway.

The score was 4–2 with one more inning left to play.
First base was the front tire of a broken-down Chevrolet.

Second base was a manhole, which always stayed in place.
Third base was a piece of cardboard found in steeplechase.

The sewer cover was home plate.
Each team was anxious to win and celebrate.

It was a rival game between Herzl and Amboy Street that was played
once a year.
Since there was no more room on the steps,
people took out their folding chair.

Some fans watching from their stoops found
it more exciting than reading

the Amboy Dukes!

Garbage cans were lined up, so cars weren't permitted to enter.
Someone yelled out to a noisy old lady, "Be quiet, you yenta!"

My Brooklyn, My Way

It was in the summer of '56, and the game started at
three. Everyone was ready, including the referee.

The score was chalked on the asphalt, where everyone could see.
It was now the final inning, and Amboy needed three.

And then when Heshy was thrown out at first, and Motkin did the same,
a silence fell upon some Brooklynites that were watching the game.

A number of neighbors got up leaving in despair. The rest sat on
their stoops and fire escapes, hoping Moshe could appear.

Moshe was the best hitter on their team.
He had both power, brains, and self-esteem.

The rubber ball they used was pinkish in color.
The bat was a broomstick handle taken from the
kitchen from another player's mother.

They thought if only Eugene and Myron could get on base, then Moshe
could connect and hit three sewers and putting that ball in space.

So upon that stricken multitude grim melancholy sat,
for there seemed but little chance of Moshe getting to bat.

But Myron let drive a single, to the wonderment of all.
And Eugene, the much despised, tore the fuzz off the ball.

And when the dust had lifted, and fans saw what occurred,
there was Eugene safe at second and Myron a-hugging third.
Nobody could believe their eyes, and nobody said a word.

Then the families on Amboy Street rose giving a lusty yell.
They were louder than Ms. Cherichetti, who always rang her bell.

It rumbled through the candy store then rattled the grocery too.
It pounded on the rooftop and recoiled upon the brick.
For now, Moshe, mighty Moshe, had picked up that broomstick.

My Brooklyn, My Way

There was ease in Moshe's manner as he stepped into his place.
There was pride in Moshe's bearing, and a smile lit Moshe's face.

And when, responding to the cheers, his mom passed him a Yarmaka to replace his hat,
no stranger in the crowd could doubt 'twas Moshe "at the bat."

Hundreds of eyes were on him as he rubbed his hands with dirt;
one hundred tongues applauded when he wiped it on his shirt.

Then while the Herzl Street pitcher ground the Spaldeen to his hip,
defiance flashed in Moshe's eye; a sneer curled Moshe's lip.

Now the pitcher threw a knuckleball that bounced like a bun.
Moshe said that "ain't my style," and the umpire said, "Strike 1."

From the stoops and the windows, there went a muffled roar,
like the beating of the storm waves on the Coney Island shore.

"Kill him! Kill the umpire!" shouted a father from the stand.
And it's likely they'd have killed him, but
Murder Incorporated was not on hand.

He signaled to the pitcher, and that Spaldeen stopped then flew.
But Moshe still ignored it, and the umpire said, "Strike 2!"

"Fraud!" cried the maddened neighbors, and they all started to scream.
But Moshe was not out yet, and his eyes still had that gleam.

They saw his face grow stern and cold; they saw his payees curl.
And all knew there was no chance he would not give that ball a whirl.

His mom said, "Moshe you need a nosh," she sent over a glass of borscht
with a matzah ball. I'm sure that combination raised his cholesterol.

His mom said she did a mitzvah then said a prayer or two.
All the fans applauded and said, "Moshe, you are now a Kosher Jew."

My Brooklyn, My Way

The sneer is gone from Moshe's lip.
His teeth are clenched in hate.
He knew he had to be the pursuer,
So he pounded his bat on the sewer.

And now the pitcher holds the ball, and now he lets it go.
And now the air is shattered by the force of Moshe's blow.

Oh, somewhere in this favored land the sun is shining bright,
the band is playing "Hava Nagila," and somewhere hearts are light.

And somewhere men are laughing, and somewhere teams have won.
But now there's joy on Amboy Street—
Moshe "the mensch" hit a home run.

Baseball

Growing up in Brooklyn, the sport everyone spoke about was baseball. In Brownsville, the Brooklyn Dodgers were always the main topic. Because it was a Jewish neighborhood, a topic that would come up constantly was who the Jewish ballplayers were. There weren't too many, but there were players over the years who excelled in this national pastime. The blacks, like Jackie Robinson, as well as the Jewish players, faced much prejudice. Robinson was a professional baseball player who became the first African American to play in Major League Baseball. He broke the baseball color line when the Brooklyn Dodgers started him at first base in 1947. There was always conversation about how Robinson would drive the pitchers crazy when he was on base. He not only was fast but also knew how to take those few extra steps to advance on the bases.

My dad used to talk about Jewish baseball players like Hank Greenberg, nicknamed the Hebrew Hammer, who was an American Major League first baseman in the 1930s and 1940s. I remember reading a nostalgic documentary about Hank as a baseball player who transcended religious prejudice to become an American icon.

There were players like Al Rosen and even Jake Pitler, who would not play on the field during the high holidays. There were always many conversations about some great Jewish players. In later years, there were great Jewish players like Sandy Koufax, Shawn Green, and Ron Bloomberg, and not long ago, an article came out that Ralph Branca's mom was Jewish, which makes him Jewish.

There is one player whom my dad spoke about that I've never seen play, and that was Sid Gordon (1917–1975). His nickname was the Solid Ballplayer. He played with the New York Giants, the Boston and Milwaukee

113

Braves, and the Pittsburgh Pirates. It was just too bad he didn't play for Brooklyn; the fans would have gone wild. He played thirteen years in the majors with an all-time 283 batting average. He hit over 200 home runs and had over 800 RBIs.

It just so happens that my dad watched Sid Gordon play baseball at Betsy Head Park. He was in a baseball league two blocks from my house on Amboy Street. I was told at one time, he hit one ball into the Betsy Head Pool that had to be at least five hundred feet. I was probably in the pool at that time and happy the ball did not hit me. He was born in Brownsville, Brooklyn. His parents were Morris and Rose (Meyerson) Gordon, who emigrated from Russia. His father became a plumber and then a coal dealer. Sid went to Samuel Tilden High School, the same high school three of my brothers went to, where he was a star baseball player.

I Remember Stickball

The game that I excelled in was stickball. I was able to hit that ball farther than two sewers. Even though I was not tall in stature, I did lift weights I received from a relative, Artie Cohen. I had nice-sized muscles, and I would roll up my short-sleeve undershirt to show off. It looked better than my rolled up cuffs.

It may seem very strange, but recently as I was watching one of my favorite TV shows, *American Pickers*, Frank and Mike noticed an old garbage can while scavenging through the attic during their search for some hidden treasures. They paid hundreds of dollars for that can. These were the same cans that lined the sidewalks of Amboy Street. They were short, always dented, and made from reinforced steel. They were also used to store coal before oil took over heating our homes. That may be the reason they were also called ash cans. It brought up memories of my childhood, and I started to reminisce about stickball in the '50s.

Before we were ready to choose sides for a stickball game, we would line up the garbage cans at the end of the street, preventing cars from entering, making sure they wouldn't interfere with our game. We would play seven on a side. The best players who were picked first were judged on their power. The ball of choice was the Spaldeen, or correctly spelled Spaldeen. We would use an old broom handle, which was taped to get a good grip. One popular place it was played was in the middle of the gutter. If you took a good swing and connected that ball would go far..

First base was usually the front tire of a parked car. Second base was the manhole in the middle of the street. Third base was a paper carton, and home plate was another manhole cover. Since there were always a few cars parked on the street, you had to be a good fielder because they had to maneuver between parked cars.

Moms and dads would be watching the game, looking out their windows. Neighbors would be sitting on their stoops. This was a typical summer day in Brooklyn. There was cheering, and the moms of my friends would yell out the windows to put on a sweater because it was starting to rain. The game would last seven innings. Balls were lost on the roofs and fences, and many windows were broken, but the games continued through the night if the game went into extra innings.

Sometimes, the ball would roll into an open sewer, and many times, it was too deep to fish up the ball. But with our imagination we would always figure out a way to retrieve the ball. I remember a small young boy we called the sewer rat that we would hold by his feet and lower him in the sewer headfirst. When he came up with the ball in his hand, everyone would clap.

It was also played in the schoolyard, where you would paint a square on the wall. By doing this, you eliminated the catcher. You would use chalk to make a rectangle on a wall. The pitcher had the best view and called the the balls and strikes. If there was a dispute, you would examine the ball for chalk marks. That was better than today's instant replay

Brooklyn Dodgers

I was a Brooklyn Dodgers fan. I remember when I was a young teenager walking with my friends down Amboy Street on hot summer nights, passing by the buildings with stoops crowded with neighbors listening to the Brooklyn Dodgers on their radios. It seemed the bums would always lose the game in the final innings, and everyone in the streets would say, "Wait till next year." That year came in 1955, when they beat the Yankees in seven games for the first championship in franchise history. A few years later, they moved to LA and took away those wonderful evenings of people sitting on the stoops.

When the Brooklyn Dodgers were playing, we would ask the score every few homes we passed. If a player like Jackie Robinson would get a hit or steal a base, there was always a fifteen-minute conversation on baseball. Pee Wee Reese was a great clutch player always coming through with a hit when we needed it.

During those years, I happened to go to many Dodger games with my friends. The reason why we went so often was the Borden Ice Cream Company ran a promotion. If you collected ten paper Elsie's Ice Cream wrappers, you could attend a Dodger game and sit in the bleachers free of charge. My friends and I would walk around the street looking for that picture of the cow. We even looked in garbage cans, anything for a free visit to watch a Brooklyn Dodger game at Ebbets Field.

When we got to the bleachers, we would sneak down to the box seats, where our neighbor Larry, who was a mailman and my father's friend, worked part time as an usher for Ebbets Field. What a great upgrade. Now when you attend a game, expect to pay a few hundred dollars, and that doesn't include an Elsie's ice cream pop.

My Brooklyn, My Way

On April 18, 1958, the Los Angeles Dodgers played their first game in LA. Just about every fan from Brooklyn lost interest, especially in the Dodgers because they were abandoned by the owner, Walter O'Malley. He wanted to move his team west, where the city of Los Angeles had agreed to build him a new stadium, and Brooklyn refused. It all had to do with money. And even though the Brooklyn fans were always loyal and never gave up hope, it did not mean a thing. Now my friends and I would not have to search the streets for Elsie wrappers. It was a sad day for Brooklyn. Sadly, their catcher, Roy Campanella, was left partially paralyzed in an off-season automobile accident on January 28, 1958. He was never able to play for Los Angeles.

Post Office (Poem)

by Martin Lewis Blumberg

There was a young boy that was really a joy
He did have a rule, never to forget his lunch
when he went to school.

When lunchtime came
and he started to look, he realized his backpack
was empty except for a book.

He went home hungry and couldn't wait to snack.
He noticed the pantry empty but saw some cans in the back.
When climbing on the chair, he realized something
was not very clear.

The cans said "Dog Food," which he was able to read, but
his family had no pets, especially not a dog to feed. He was puzzled
and confused
and just didn't know why there was so much dog food but not
even a slice of pie.

When his mom came home, he didn't want to be rude, but he asked her
why there
was so much dog food.

She said she just went shopping and bought plenty
for him to eat. She then filled up his plate with many a treat.

As he was eating, she started to say why there was
dog food in the pantry each and every day.

She explained since his dad was a mailman, he had plenty to fear. There were
many a stray dogs that would run to him, bark, and give him a scare. So your dad
would feed these dogs treats that he kept in his bag. He would notice the dogs'
tails begin to wag.

"So now, my son, you have the answer, and I hope you understand
that your father does his job the best way that he can.
He makes sure the mail is delivered so it gets there on time,
and I am sure, son, you'll agree that's surely not a crime."

Canarsie History

Canarsie pier

The first people recorded who settled in Brooklyn was an Indian tribe called the Canarsie Indians. In the middle of the seventeenth century, the Dutch West India Company established permanent residence and took over the territory. In the early twentieth century, there was an area called the "Golden City," which was a popular amusement park that burned to the ground. It was like Coney Island with rides and attractions. The Bayview projects were being built right in that spot, a block from Canarsie pier.

Getting Ready for Canarsie

The year was 1956, and I was in the first graduating class of David Marcus JHS, PS 263. Along with all my friends from Amboy Street, I was looking forward to attending Tilden High School. Being a teenager was great. In fact, I realized that there were other things in this world besides Spaldeens- like girls. Little did I know that my parents signed up to be tenants in a new housing project in Canarsie, Brooklyn, called Bayview. The New York City Housing Authority had applications for families who earned a certain low income. This development was big. It had twenty-three eight-story buildings with over 1,600 apartments and was to be completed in June 1956.

Since my dad was a mailman and never earning a big salary, our family qualified. Not only that but also we were ready for a new lifestyle. I just couldn't imagine moving to a new building on the sixth floor, with an elevator, and with a view of Canarsie Bay in the distance. All I ever knew was living on the ground floor, and the only view was watching the water spray out of the fire hydrant.

I never thought that day would come when we would move from a ghetto to a palace. Tears came to my eyes knowing my parents have accomplished so much with so little. But there was love, hard work, smiles, and prayers that elevated them to this point. My parents, who never looked for material things, gave us the closeness and love that really mattered. Their main concerns were earning an honest living and making sure there was food on the table and their children would have a good education. Now with all their hard work, they were rewarded.

My mom would now have a new kitchen with new appliances and a bathroom with a sink. This is more than anyone could ask for. Now I could share a bedroom with one of my brothers, and, yes, I did not need to open the sofa every night and pile books under the broken leg.

But best of all, my mom would be away from the coal that poured into our cellar contaminating the air that my family had to breathe each day.

I had some second thoughts knowing I would leave my friends. I would be going to Jefferson, and the kids still living on Amboy were going to Tilden. I realized I would miss the corner candy store and the grocery store person who was able to trust our family until the end of the week. I would also miss playing in the streets and, of course, my second home, Betsy Head Pool. I would miss the seltzer man and the throwing of money to the man playing the violin in my alleyway. But I was ready for the change. Brownsville was starting to get worse, not better.

I was ready for the transition knowing Canarsie was not at the end of the world, and hopefully, I would still be in contact with my friends. Fortunately, it all worked out. Not only did I meet new friends but also my friends from Amboy Street kept in contact. They would even hitchhike to Canarsie. My memories of Brownsville are still with me and will always be with me. I'll never forget that. It brings to mind my humble upbringing and the happiness it gave me. But most of all, my mother and father lived a much longer, healthier, and happier life knowing they did the right thing for their children.

In 1958, my family moved from Amboy Street to the Bayview Projects in Canarsie. My friends from Amboy Street would visit me often, and they would hang around with my new friends. We were about eighteen-year-old high school seniors and juniors from Jefferson and Tilden. Since I lived close to the Belt Parkway, we would break up into groups of four and hitchhike to Coney Island.

Canarsie, My New Home

View from our Bayview apartment 6F (1958)

*C*anarsie was a fun place to live. Bayview was a new development and most of my friends came from different parts of Brooklyn. Many of the boys and girls came from Brownsville. It was easy to make friends and meet girls because we all came from similar backgrounds.

The playgrounds on Seaview Avenue were always filled with kids playing. The schoolyard was a short distance away from 2045 Rockaway Parkway, my new address, and just like Amboy Street, there were always softball or basketball games being played. We even had a brick wall in our schoolyard, where we would chalk up a home plate to play stickball.

We moved to apartment 6F, and even though it was impossible for my mom to talk to people passing by, she still looked out the window with that same rock pillow under her arms. Our new telephone number was CL1-5050 and without a party line. My two elder brothers were married and already served in the army, so with three bedrooms, we had plenty of privacy. My two brothers Jack and Bruce also made lots of friends. Since I still had my friends visit me from Brownsville, it was easy for me to adjust to my new lifestyle.

Lloyd 60

The Bayview Project was a great place to live. I still had my friends from Amboy Street and now new friends in Canarsie. I took the Pioneer bus to Jefferson or the train to Livonia Avenue. I would walk past Fortunoff, which was a few blocks from TJHS. My friends from Amboy Street would visit me in Canarsie, and by introducing them to my new friends, I created a bond.

I came up with the idea to start a club where all my friends would join together as one group. All I needed was a name for the club and a clubhouse. One of my friends got a tip that a Mrs. Kline, who owned a home at 650 Osborn Street, was looking to rent out her basement. With so many guys, we could chip in a few dollars each month. That was not a problem. It was already furnished with two couches that when you sat in them, you sank to the floor and couldn't get up. The name of our club was taken from my elder brothers' fraternity from City College who were graduating in 1960. The name Lloyd 60 sounded very collegiate; hence, the name Lloyd 60 became our name.

There were many high school sororities in Brooklyn with many groups of girls who would travel to meet boys at different fraternities. I was voted social director and was ready to rock and roll. I would call different girls and invite them to our club, and when I said Lloyd 60, they thought we were college students, not realizing we were high school seniors. It was a success. Groups of girls flocked to Osborn Street. They lined up outside the club. Many of the girls left noticing the guys were their age, but many stayed, and many of my friends married girls who came to our socials.

Many girls wore hot pink jackets, powder blue jackets, or sweaters with their names on the front with their group name in big letters on the back.

My Brooklyn, My Way

Nobody showed up on Saturday (that would show they did not have a date), but Friday nights were packed. Every Brooklyn High School had some groups of sororities that wanted to hang out and meet guys (especially college guys).

I had one friend who had a big collection of 45s with the songs of the '50s—songs that I knew every word and still remember today. There were words that I had no idea what it meant like Fats Domino's "Tutti Frutti." But there were songs like "I Ran All the Way Home" by the Impalas, how a guy ran all the way home just to say he's sorry. Today, they could have texted it without getting out of breath.

We started the music with the stroll, walking through the cellar steps, down the aisle with some crazy moves. During the week, we would watch *American Bandstand* with Dick Clark. I loved to watch them dance the lindy (Philly style).

The next songs were fast songs like Bill Haley's "Rock around the Clock." By the time the slow dances started, the lights became dimmer and dimmer. We would explain to girls that were paired off with my friends that the landlord (Mrs. Kline) was complaining the electric bill was too high.

Then came the slow songs like "Earth Angel" by the Penguins or "Only You" by the Platters. By the time Frank Sinatra was played, the lights were off completely, and we sat on the couch to make out. Again, we blamed it on Mrs. Kline. But it was too late. Once they were on the couches, they could not get up.

After an hour, it was time for the card game. We took phone numbers and showed them the door and told them we would call for a Saturday night date, and they went home without a chaperone.

One of my friends came up with an idea to have what we called "Pig Night." We would all ask a girl out for a date. These were girls that were never asked out. We thought it would be a nice gesture since these girls were unattractive and never asked on a date. We were to award a trophy to the guy that brought the least attractive girl. I don't know where they found some of these girls. Two of my friends picked up their dates that weighed about two hundred pounds each. As he drove down the street, sparks were everywhere because the tailpipe of the car was being dragged on the gutter. When the girls arrived, the two heavyweights sat on our couch. That became a problem because that's where they were the whole night because that couch was so low to the ground, they were not able to get up. The funny part about the story was one of my friends was going steady, and since he was not allowed to date because he gave his girlfriend an ankle bracelet, he had to take her, he won but we were to embarrassed to award him the trophy.

Lloyd 60 members

Myron Antonoff
Martin Blumberg
Michael Charney
Aaron Cutler
David Friedman
Melvin Goldberg
Heshy Goldstein
Steven Kapelner
Stanley Kirtman
Howie Fink (Rauchwerger)
Eugene Shaw
Larry Wexler

Our Lloyd 60 Clubhouse at 650 Osborn Street (1958)

Coney Island

Hanging out with my friends in Brighton Beach trying to pick up girls. Myron standing in a hole did not help (1959)

There was a lot to do on Coney Island. It was always crowded both at the beach and the amusement park. During the day, our choice of beaches was Bay 4 in Brighton. In the evening, we go to Surf Avenue and spend the evening walking around Coney Island. A few dollars in those days went a long way. There were so many rides and also arcades to keep you busy. Some of the rides we went on were the Virginia reel, Caterpillar ride, Bobsled, Ferris wheel, Parachute Drop, Wonder Wheel, Cyclone, Tornado roller coaster, and I could go on and on. I remember my friends would all take out bumper cars and crash into one another, trying to take them out of action. We would even turn around and attempt a head-on collision. We were not required to wear helmets, but nobody ever got hurt.

We never visited Steeplechase Park because that required an extra cost. I do recall looking watching the Pony ride race through a hole in the fence. We had more than enough activities to keep us busy. And of course, we had to save some money for a hot dog and french fries at Nathan's Famous.

When we walked down Surf Avenue, we stopped at many arcades. I remember taking a photo with all my friends in a booth the size of a telephone booth. The pictures would be produced instantly on black-and-white film about a foot long. With a cost of twenty-five cents, we were able to record our own 33 RPM record with a personalized label. I remember passing poker-playing monkeys that were in the window of the World of Wax. We would stare in the window watching chimpanzees playing poker and cheating. We were able to see cards hidden up their sleeves.

Then there were the sideshows. We would stop in front of a stand. There was a barker telling about the show. There were crowds of people who would gather in front. They would tease you to come in for an entrance fee. I remember the lady who came out and swallowed a sword and the tattoo lady (today that's all you see). There were fire eaters, the tallest man, and the smallest man—you name it, they had it. It was an experience to stand and listen to the barker draw people inside. Each act was its own attraction, but we never entered. I recall them having patrons called "planters" which after the presentation they would walk to the window to get tickets. We knew they were set up because they would enter after every show.

I remember going with my parents for dinner at Carolina's on Mermaid Avenue and on West Fifteenth Street, a great Italian restaurant with tuxedo-clad waiters serving the best old-school Italian food called Gargiulo's. One of the owners, who weighed about three hundred pounds, would walk to our table with the bill. He told us to pick a number. He would rattle a bowl with numbers, and if that was the number you picked, your bill was free. We were not that lucky.

Today, the old site of the Steeplechase Park is occupied by Minor League Baseball team. Landmarks like the Parachute Jump are not being used but still exist. Nathan's Famous is still selling the best frankfurters.

Over the years, Coney Island has deteriorated, but there has been a revitalization. It's hard for one to imagine if it will ever be the same. But Coney Island, despite its problems, is an area with so much potential and carries a strong part of the spirit and culture of Brooklyn. It has beautiful beaches and a wonderful history. It was one of the coolest places I visited as a child. I just hope our next generation can experience and appreciate the beauty Coney Island has to offer.

I Ran All the Way Home

Speedo and the Impalas - I ran all the way home (1958)

I was friends with a black kid who lived in the Bayview project named Joe Frazier. He was a good basketball player but never passed. Every time he got the ball, he would shoot. We would play half court, three on a side. There was always another group waiting in the wings to play the winners. There was always a new team waiting that would call, "Next," which gave them the right to play the winner. I always picked him on my team, because he was a great shooter. He loved to drive in for layups. If he missed, he would call a foul. That was a sure way to win.

At night, we would listen to Joe with a doo-wop group that consisted of three other guys. They had a good sound, would harmonize different songs, and would practice at a candy store on the corner. Joe was the lead singer. They wrote most of their own music. Joe's nickname was Speedo, and they called themselves the Impalas.

In 1958, they signed with Cub records, and the next year, they released their first song called "Sorry (I Ran All the Way Home)," which scored high on the charts and became a hit. Unfortunately, no further hits ever came, and they were considered a one-song wonder.

Later in years, I went with my wife, Maxine, to see the group perform at Jones Beach at a concert. Before the performance, I walked up to Speedo and asked if he remembered me from the projects and the basketball games we played in Bayview. He did recognize me and said he remembered our three-on-three games, but I never passed him the ball. I guess he was joking. Before the concert, he made an announcement, dedicating the song "Sorry" to Marty Blumberg. That was nostalgia at its best.

People from Bayview

My younger brother Bruce made good friends in Canarsie that he is still in contact with Lou Vairo who was head coach for the men's Olympic hockey team. He became assistant coach for the New Jersey Devils and was inducted in the United States Hockey Hall of Fame. Lou lived in our building in the Bayview projects.

John Brockington, who was an all-pro quarterback with the Green Bay Packers coached under Vince Lambardi, also lived in the Bayview Projects. My brother Bruce spent a good portion of his early years as very close friends, and even today they keep in contact.

Another talent from Bayview was Steven Keats, a professional actor who was in several movies like *Death Wish*. Bruce played in the Little League with Steve. Steve is now deceased.

Bob Hartstein was one of the best high school basketball coaches in the country. He coached basketball at Lincoln High School. He spent a good portion of his earlier years being very close friends with my brother Bruce along with Neil Steinberg, who was the assistant coach at Lincoln.

I remember reading in the newspapers that Hartstein saved a student from committing suicide during his coaching years.

He coached several players who went on to the NBA, including Stephon Marbury, who was the first-round fourth pick in the 1996 NBA draft who went on to become an NBA all star for several seasons.

Howard Schultz, who founded Starbucks, lived in Bayview near our schoolyard. When he appeared on CBS's *60 minutes*, less than a year ago, he mentioned in his narrative that he was considering running for president. That would have been interesting, a Jewish boy from Canarsie becoming president. But he changed his mind pretty fast. He also mentioned how he came from a low-income project called Bayview and lived at the lowest level. But not to the Blumberg's, Bayview was a utopia compared to Amboy Street. Bayview was a middle income project, not low. I am sure if he came from Brownsville and passed our window on Amboy Street, my mom would offer him a cup of A&P coffee along with a cookie from our cookie jar. I just wonder before he would take a bite of that cookie, would he sniff it first like Annie Hunk did?

Mike Tyson from Amboy Street

I truly believe that life is not only luck and being in the right place at the right time, but I feel that fate has a lot to do with the outcome of one's destiny. I believe that the development of certain events in one's life, is beyond a person's control. If I was born 20 years earlier or twenty years later my life would have been completely different. Being born in Brownsville in 1941 has made my journey through life a memorable experience.

When I look at a person like Mike Tyson, who was one of the greatest boxing champions, I understand his upbringing was so much different from mine even though we were brought up on the same street. When "Iron Mike "was seven, his family settled at 178 Amboy Street in the Brownsville section of Brooklyn, a few buildings away from where I was raised. We moved twenty years prior, and I understand the surrounding area got much worse after we moved. Amboy Street was decaying to a point where poverty and crime became prevalent. At that time Brownsville was considered the most dangerous section in Brooklyn.

Stealing became a way of life for Mike and before he was eleven years of age he was drinking, and smoking marijuana. There was no more ball playing on Amboy Street because the street were in disarray. Tyson was arrested over forty times before he reached twelve. But, what if Tyson was born twenty years earlier? I am sure his life would have been much different. With his power I'm sure he would have been a great stickball player. I could picture my mom offering Tyson a hot meal as he past our apartment.

But, I give give Tyson credit for growing up on Amboy Street in the worst conditions, and succeeding in securing a permanent place for himself in the annals of boxing.

My Philosophy of Memories

My childhood is packed with memories of events and activities that have touched my life as well as my family and friends. I believe these memories have shaped me into the person I am today. Every day, the best scientists around the world collaborate to unravel the mysteries of the human mind and try to understand how the brain works and its effects with memories. I feel that past events from my childhood have influenced my everyday life.

When I think back to the many memories I have, there is one in particular that seems never to fade, and that's my Brooklyn childhood years. When I reminisce and think about those past events, I truly think that my childhood was one of the happiest times of my life, maybe because life was carefree and easy. I didn't have to make important decisions, and as a child, I was always excited and enthusiastic about the activities I was participating in. There were few responsibilities compared with what an adult has to endure in everyday life.

I think about my memories of my childhood years growing up in Brooklyn. These memories are clear even though I'm seventy-eight years old. When I try to understand the brain and the way one is able to recollect things that happened over seventy-five years ago, it becomes puzzling. My belief is when one experiences life, they take pictures not with cameras but with their eyes and minds. These pictures are then transformed from our thoughts and eyes to our brains; that's where we keep them stored. I am fortunate to be able to bring up these memories and visualize these pictures, which are clear as can be, in today's world. Even though my memories are stored in my brain, I am still able to visualize these thoughts that are embedded in my everyday actions, along with my memories.

My Brooklyn, My Way

I feel our brains, essentially, are like today's computers with our consciousness like a computer program. It could not run when the computer is turned off or when we die, but as long as we're alive, we can bring up what is stored with our minds just like a memory chip. Theoretically, it could be recreated on a neural network, but that would be very difficult because of the vast amount of memories one has stored in their brains.

When these memories are encoded in our brains, it becomes a "wiring diagram," which makes up one's personality that makes us unique. Your memory is formed by neurons in your brain, which retains information from certain events, and when you press the right key, you could bring up that memory. I feel fortunate knowing where these keys are situated, and it's all thanks to my typing teacher, Mr. Rappaport, from Junior High School, who constantly repeated these keys.

I truly believe people who have fond memories of childhood, specifically their relationships with their parents and siblings, tend to have better health, less depression, and fewer chronic diseases when they get older. I also feel the older we get, our days pass by at a much faster rate than when we were younger, and in most cases, our short-term memories fade, just like mine did.

My memory plays a huge part in how I judge a situation, and it's much more than a simple escape from reality. It shows me how much I've grown as a person because of my wonderful past and childhood.

We Met at a Dance

On March 14, 2019, my wife and I celebrated fifty-five years of a happy and great marriage. Time has gone very fast, and my wife and I were truly blessed to have a close and beautiful family. Both being in our seventies, it just doesn't seem possible. We thank God that we and our family are healthy and that we both still feel young.

The story about how I met my wife is an interesting one, and I would like to share it with you. I recall it like it was yesterday about how I got the attention of my future wife, Maxine, when we met at a dance.

My friends and I decided to go to a dance at a Jewish Center in Rego Park, Queens, in 1961. We lived in Canarsie, Brooklyn, at that time. When I got there, I saw this beautiful girl talking to her friends and asked her to dance. She told me her name was Maxine. She was sixteen and lived in Forest Hills.

I said, "You moved recently." She said, "Yes, how did you know?" It was just a guess, but I didn't tell her that. I wanted to pique her curiosity because although I was only twenty, I knew immediately that she was the person I wanted to share my life with.

As we danced, I continued guessing and said, "You have a brother, and you just broke up with a boyfriend." I was right again. After a few dances, I went back to my friends on the other side of the room. I was playing hard to get. Sometime later, Maxine walked over to me, asking again how I knew those things about her. I kept her guessing.

After the last dance, I asked if I could walk her home, and she agreed. On the way, we stopped at Jahn's Ice Cream Parlor on Queens Boulevard. Maxine was a junior in high school. I was working during the day and attending evening classes at Brooklyn College.

My Brooklyn, My Way

When we got to her doorstep, I leaned over to kiss her. She put up her hand and said, "I do not kiss on the first date." I said, "Let's make believe it's our last date." She went along with that and let me give her a little peck on the cheek.

A few days later, I called her and we began dating. Every Friday night, we would eat Chinese food at a place called Sunny's on Queens Boulevard in Forest Hills.

I remember taking her on some exotic dates, like night court in downtown Brooklyn, where we'd listen to different cases. When it was a nice night, we'd ride back and forth on the Staten Island Ferry. I told her not to get off the ferry when it pulled into Staten Island because it would have cost ten cents to get back on. As you can see, these were not expensive dates. We'd sometimes take in a movie or double-date with friends.

I have been very fortunate to have lived a wonderful life, not only in my childhood years but also in today's world. I was blessed to have found the best soulmate any person could ask for. Maxine and I were able to experience this magnificent journey together. We have three marvelous children and, along with their spouses, they've given us 10 wonderful grandchildren.

I'm still in love with that girl I noticed across the dance floor more than 55 years ago. You may say that knowing things about her was a lucky guess, but I say it was fate and it was all meant to be. But, I also have to thank my mom. After I got home from that dance, my mom was up and she asked me if I had a nice time. I told her I met a very pretty girl that lives in Forest Hills. I told her that when I walked her home, I noticed a doorman and an elevator in her apartment building.

My mom's immediate response was, "marry her."

After dating for more than two years, I asked Maxine's mom permission to marry her daughter. I said; "I love your daughter and would like your approval to marry her." Her response was "No, she could do better." Can you imagine how we felt? But that didn't stop us. We were married at "Leonard's of Great Neck" on March 14, 1964.

A funny story that I like to tell is that over the years, many people have asked me how I knew so many things about Maxine during that first dance. I would tell them, "If you danced with 25 girls and told them all the same things, I am sure you'll be correct on at least one girl." That's a joke, Maxine! I danced only with you that night.

Maxine retired in 2008 as an account executive with Studebaker-Worthington leasing company in Jericho. I retired in 2012 from our family-run auto parts store called Auto Barn.

When I reminisce and look back on the beautiful years we have shared, it brings joy to my heart. These fifty-five years of marriage were beyond our greatest dreams. Who said marriage doesn't work?

Fact: We have ten grandchildren that includes three sets of twins!

We should both be in "Ripley's Believe It or Not" for having three sets of twin grandchildren:

>Samantha and Eliza (two girls), twenty years old
>Max and Miriam (boy and girl), ten years old
>Connor and Brody (two boys), three years old

Maxine and I celebrating my 75th birthday (2016)

The Remote

For the first few years of marriage, I would always watch TV with my wife. But over the years, things have changed. It's very rare for us to watch TV together. It was not the TV that separated us; I blame it on the remote control, which I call the clicker. In the beginning, we would enjoy the same shows and seldom got up to change the channels. It seemed easier to relax and then to walk five feet to our television set to change the station.

I was brought up watching a few stations and never needed a clicker. But when the remote was invented and my wife got it in her own hands, it gave her the power, and she took control. She would go from channel to channel in a few seconds, and over time, it became overwhelming. When I got home from work, after dinner, I needed this time to unwind and relax. With that clicker in her hand, she had the power at her fingertips and loved it. She never really asked me what I wanted to watch, and eventually, we did not enjoy the same shows.

I could turn on a sports event like baseball, even golf, and watch it for hours. I even watched the commercials, never changing the station. But not my wife; she could watch *The Real Housewives of New York*, *The Real Housewives of Beverly Hills*, *Frasier*, and the news all at the same time, never missing a line. I don't think she ever watched a commercial in her life.

So for the last thirty years, I have been going into another room, where I could watch the shows I love and not worry about the changing of a channel during an important program. I became king of my own set. There is nothing worse than missing a sentence from a show by flipping that remote.

Sometimes if I want to be romantic, I go into the room she is watching her show. I sit down next to her trying to show interest in what she is watching. The only problem is that the show turns out to be boring, and inevitably I fall asleep. I am sure she realizes it, but I wake up when she'll ask me a question about the show. I usually answer her by changing the subject or saying "I love you." She'll smile and change the station, and I'll fall back to sleep.

Family picture with my wife Maxine, with our children Stacey, Richard, and Felicia (2018)

I Do the Shopping

For the past fifty years, my wife did all the shopping. Yes, there were many times I would follow her around the supermarket. I never paid much attention, but I do recall her reading the labels, checking sodium, and even checking the weights on the packages. She would buy mostly the sale items on her list.

Occasionally, I would suggest that she buy extra Campbell's split pea soup since I love pea soup. I never wanted to be without it. She would check the coupons she kept in an envelope, and if she did not have one for that item, she would tell me to wait until it goes on sale. I never enjoyed going with her because it seemed she just took me along just to push the cart, empty it into the car, and when we got home, to bring everything into the house.

In the house, my main job was to take out the garbage. I knew exactly which days the garbage truck would come, and I would wheel the cans to the curb, making sure the lids were tight. I think I did a pretty good job since I have not had a complaint in fifty years.

For some reason, for the last six months, I have taken on a new job. My wife asked me to assume this task of food shopping. I remembered my mom giving me a shopping list when I lived in Brownsville, which I brought to the corner grocery store. Even though he helped, I always brought home the right stuff. I also knew how I mastered taking out the garbage. I would have no problem doing the food shopping.

My wife said she would help me by giving me the circular and checking off the sale items and providing me with the coupons. She would also write down other items. Since I have been retired for a number of years, I knew I could find the time to help her.

My Brooklyn, My Way

I was ready to take on this challenge. But when I walked into the supermarket all alone, it looked like the size of a football stadium. I was all set to leave, but I got enough courage when I realized how I mastered the garbage. I then said to myself, "Marty, you can do it." I then looked around and noticed aisle number one. I said to myself that would be a good place to start; it turned out to be a nightmare.

I had no idea what I was doing. My wife's handwriting was in hieroglyphics. I had no idea what she wrote. Who knew that TP meant toilet paper? I bought toothpicks. It took me more than two hours to buy all the wrong stuff.

I bought no-fat milk when she wanted 2 percent. Whatever happened to just plain homogenized milk? I purchased regular coffee when she circled decaf. She never told me to move each egg in the carton; four were cracked. I never even opened the carton. I never knew there was detergent with bleach and one for colored clothes.

I never should have started on aisle one. That was where the ice cream was. It was dripping as I walked into our kitchen. The rotisserie chicken that was in aisle two was ice-cold. When I opened the door, my wife was dialing the police to find out if I was dead. She sent me back, and since we were starving, I returned the order, and we had to eat out.

But now things have changed. After bringing home the wrong items for another month, I think my wife has changed me into a robot. Now when I go into the supermarket, I have no control of what I am doing. Unconsciously, I go right to an aisle. After taking ten steps, I turn to the right. Putting out my hand, I bend down three inches and pull a box of cereal off the shelf. I know by the size of the box and the picture that it is the right item. I then go to the next isle, I then take twenty-two steps and reach out for those paper towels. I know PT means paper towels.

The last items I buy are the ice cream and chicken. I am so proud of my achievements. When I arrived home, the chicken was burning hot, ready to eat. I now wait for that seldom compliment from my wife that I got everything right. But, no, she says, "Marty, you forgot to take out the garbage." Can you believe it? I forgot.

Take me back to the good old days. Take me back to my childhood in Brooklyn, where there was never a worry and the local grocer would take care of all the shopping.

Taking a Swing at Golf

After my retirement more than nine years ago, I decided to take up the game of golf. I knew nothing about the game. As a matter of fact, in the beginning, I would pack an extra pair of trousers in my bag, just in case I got a hole in one.

But now at the age of seventy eight, I go out once a week during the warmer months with three friends—Irv, Dennis, and Ken—to the Dix Hills Park Golf Course, a nine-hole course off Commack Road that's run by the town of Huntington. We don't keep score, but we get plenty of exercise and find it both challenging and fun not using a motorized cart.

In the beginning, I took a lesson, but I was not comfortable holding the club with one thumb over the other. I solved that problem by stopping the lessons.

I know I am improving because now I am able to count my lost balls on one hand; in the beginning, I needed two hands and my left foot. But who needs to keep score anyway? I now watch the golf tournaments on TV and see the pros hit that little ball more than three hundred yards, landing it on the green. I then say to myself that it takes me three swings just to hit the ball.

The guys I play with are also retired. They do point things out to me and give me helpful hints like "Look at the ball," "Keep your head down," and "Direct your feet to the right."

Their advice seems to be working because now I am keeping up with them. I'm not saying I have high hopes or dreams of becoming a professional, but I am now ready to keep score.

My Brooklyn, My Way

I enjoy chipping and putting, and I am reminded how as a child, I always enjoyed the sand. I recently bought new irons, and with my new driver, I can hit the fairway on a regular basis.

After golfing, it's time for lunch. The main place we go is Jersey Mike's Sub on Route 110 in Farmin(ale. We all wait for Newsday, where they have a buy-one-get-one-free coupon. We all order heroes and take the free one home for lunch the next day. Since we are all retired, we do watch for specials. Sometimes, we go to the Premier Diner in Commack, where we get a 10 percent discount for being seniors.

I never heard of the game of golf in my childhood.

**Having lunch with my golf buddies,
Dennis, Ken and Irv (2018)**

Grabstein's Kosher Delicatessen

**Going back to Peter Luger with family to
a great Brooklyn Restaurant (2017)**

I remember going to Grabstein when it was on Sackman Street. My Uncle Benny lived on Powell Street and would eat out with his family once a week. My uncle's nickname was Bozzy. (I have no idea how he got that name.) I don't recall he ever drank. Because he was such a great customer of Grabstein, the owner named a steak after him called the Bozzy steak. He even put it on his menu.

Bozzy was my father's younger brother. He had two daughters. He idolized my dad for having five sons. I guess he always wanted a son because he treated all my brothers like they were his own. He invited my family for a dinner at Grabstein in the early '50s.

This was a time in its heyday when dining at the delicatessen constituted a big night. Customers were eating salami sandwiches and pickles on rye bread. Kids were eating a hot dog and sauerkraut. When you walked in, they had on each table a delicious cucumber salad. I loved specials cut in slices on club bread. I remember my dad ordering the Bozzy steak, and there was enough for my whole family to share. I can still taste that flavor of that steak.

Business started to decline in later years when many of his Jewish customers started to move out of the area. There was a continuous decline of the kosher delicatessen in many areas of Brooklyn. Even Ziggy's Deli moved from Amboy Street to a better part of Brooklyn. Grabstein was a smart businessman and had the insight to move his deli to Rockaway Parkway and Ave L, in Canarsie. He basically followed his clients where many of his customers moved to Seaview Village, which was a new development in Canarsie. I remember eating there when I lived in Bayview, and when I walked in, I noticed his cucumber salad at each table. And, yes, when I opened the menu, I noticed the Bozzy steak. I ordered a frankfurter; the steak was too expensive.

Grabsteins's delicatessen

Comments from Friends

My friend Gene Shaw from Canarsie (2015)

I met Marty Blumberg when I moved to the Bayview Projects in Canarsie. We played a lot of softball and basketball together and became very good friends. I was part of a group, (Lloyd 60) these were guys that came from Brownsville and Canarsie. I would travel to dances with Marty to pick up girls. I was there when he met his (bride to be) Maxine in Queens. I remember driving with him

My Brooklyn, My Way

in his 48 Plymouth. He wasn't sure how to get there so I volunteered to go with him on a double date with one of Maxine's friends.

After we dropped the girls off it started to snow pretty hard. While driving down Woodhaven Blvd, there was very little visibility, it was about 1:00AM and Marty stopped for a light. As soon as the light turned green his wiper blades stopped working. It was a good thing I was in the car because every few minutes he would stop, I would run out to clean the windshield. We finally made it back to Canarsie at 4AM, my hands were like ice cubes, and my date was also very cold.

—Gene Shaw

Marty Blumberg and I have been friends for over 60 years. We met in homeroom as seniors at Thomas Jefferson HS in 1958 and hit it off immediately. We had the same sense of humor and it came to pass that we came up with the idea of having a Club Room (cellar club) where we could meet girls which was a Brownsville / ENY thing. The old joke that I used to tell years later was, at Marty's Bar Mitzvah his grandmother came over to me and kissed me and gave me $20.

The club room was called Lloyd 60. We believed it would sound like we were college guys. It was located on Osborn Street near Hegeman Ave. It was an instant success. After 3 or so years we moved to East 52 Street off of Church Ave and changed the name to Rendezvous Club.

The new club room was another success but times were changing. The guys were getting older and military obligations was staring in their faces. Then President Kennedy proclaimed if you were married you were exempt. SWISH; our club house days ended.

During these several years we met lots of girls and laughed a lot. It was a wonderful time.

Finally I would like to say, new friends come and go but old friends are forever.

—Myron Antonoff

My Brooklyn, My Way

My friend Myron now living in Florida

June 23, 1941 The day I was born

Remembering my mom telling neighbors and friends, Roslyn Gene Hymowitz was 6 months old when they bombed Pearl Harbor.

Just a side note, yeah I'm 78 as is my old friends Marty Blumberg, author and Roger Elowitz, contributor––more on that soon.

A few weeks ago as the weather was warming up, I purchased a carton of Corona beer.

The checkout computer stopped, and the cashier asked for my ID.

What, you're asking me proof of age, geez the new moisturizer really works . . . so I laugh out loud and say, I was 6 months old when they bombed Pearl Harbor . . . What surprised me her question to me . . .

What's Pearl Harbor??

Right then and there, I knew we were living in much different times.

Are they not teaching American history or was she absent that day?

For me and my friends, it all started in Brownsville Brooklyn New York City Public School 175—year 1946—

Afternoon kindergarten class with Miss Porback who, at the end of the term, became our own Mrs Robinson—Marty, Roger, Dolores, Eleanor and Howard Schlectman, so many more of us . . . we have all kept in contact with each other since 1946, that's 73 remarkable years—believe me, it's not a common thing to still seek each other out, it's like yesterday—the funny stories which have been told over and over again, and not one of us has said shut up I heard it already.

Marty Blumberg sitting next to me in our brand new Junior high school with respect named for Col. David Marcus, a freedom fighter for Israel, laughing with the twinkle in his eyes, while Mr Sulman in his grey itchy suit tried to teach us math . . . actually he really did.

With all the notes passed and the comedy show in class, we all passed and continued to our revered Thomas Jefferson High School.

Backing up a wee bit, what we have accomplished as far as friendships, our parents did the same.

Both my parents were raised in Brownsville and went to PS 175.

They lived across from each other on Sutter Ave.

My dad born at home in apartment house corner Bristol St.

My mom corner Hopkinson Ave.

Their friends from school are the parents of the kids I went to school with.

Quite the magic circle.

Brownsville was our state.

Brownsville housed all our relatives which made visits special.

My Brooklyn, My Way

No telephones, maybe some had cars, but everyone was within walking distance and all it took was a knock on the door and we were company.

What a wonderful home life I had living on Bristol St.

I would walk home from school, have my Mallomars or a snowball with a glass of milk and figure out which Bubby I was going to visit.

We were smack dab in the middle 2 blocks to the right Bubby Lena, 2 blocks to the left Bubby Goldie.

Oh what joy.

And then our rite of passage: Pitkin Ave.

Going with the girlfriends to meet boyfriends—Meyers ice cream parlor and the Chocolate Shop, the seasonal treats of Charlotte Russe, Jelly Apples and a new Star "pizza."

We couldn't decide where to spend our 15 cents, a slice of pizza or a kosher frankfurter that crunched when you bit in.

I think Pizza won because they always had these Italian boys with the dark shiny Vaseline hair working... a frank we could always get, a kosher delicatessen (not deli, feh) on every block, but a hot triangle shaped slice with that insane cheese that stretched for a mile, while the oil dripped down your arm, nothing like that in Brownsville—hello new world.

And speaking of world, the year of my birth saw many of our family leave to fight a war in Europe.

Both my grandmothers said goodbye to their sons, aunts said goodbye to cousins.

The war had taken over our Brownsville with signs of Uncle Sam wants you all over.

Little American flags flew in apartment windows—signs with glitter on front doors welcoming back a soldier or sailor.

My uncle Frank, a medic in Guam, my uncle Hy stateside in Texas.

Louie #1 Navy Hawaii

Louie #2 merchant marine torpedoed in the Indian Ocean, and my dad drafted but because of his profession, stayed in New York helping to rebuild jaws and mouths of the military's devastating injuries.

He was a dental technician.

Remembering the end of the war

Going to my aunt's house on Strauss Street

Everyone was outside dancing in the street, large circles of people, and giving out corned beef sandwiches cut in half wrapped in wax paper.

Ok back to more modern times with Marty Blumberg, et al.

1956 new school and a new teacher

Mr Joe Cassius, an art teacher and a professional wrestler

He would wrestle on TV Thursday nights, and teach our art class on Fridays.

He never lost a match, he also never won a match . . . it was always a draw . . .

But it looked like he got hit in the head a few times.

So there we were, Joe Adamo (Brother)

Marty Blumberg, Marcia Miller, Johnny Pallata, all waiting to see the black and blues of Mr Cassius' face

Surprise Surprise not a mark on him

We then realized wrestling was not all cracked up to be legit unless you were Nature Boy, how's that name Marty??

We all laughed . . . did Marty and Joe high fives? I don't know—but every time we saw each other changing classes, we all had that common twinkle in our eyes.

A club, a passion to join just by having a sense of humor and that we did, til this day in the year 2020.

Boy we sure survived Animal Farm and 1984///do they still have this in print . . .

Forget about it . . . google it

Who needs to hold a book?

I do, damn it.

—Roz Hymowitz

David Marcus JHS 263 with Roger
Elowitz and Roz Hymowitz (1956)

Thomas Jefferson High School

They started to build Thomas Jefferson High School in the year of 1922. It was erected in the Brownsville section of Brooklyn at 400 Pennsylvania Avenue. Over the years, many prominent people who went there became very popular in later years. Many notable people graduated Jeff, and there were many dropouts who became famous. In 2007, the school was closed and was renamed the Thomas Jefferson Educational Campus. It specializes in a school for civil rights, FDNY Fire and Safety, performing arts, and a Community Health High School.

These are just a few of some of the graduates:

- Benjamin Lax (1915–2015), physicist elected to National Academy of Sciences
- William Levitt (1907–1994), developer of Levittown Long Island
- Norman Lloyd (born 1914), actor, director, and producer
- Norman Mailer (1923–2007), novelist, journalist, playwright, screenwriter, actor, and film director
- Mickey Marcus (1901–1948), U.S. Army colonel who became Israel's first general
- Ernest Martin (born 1932), theater director and manager, actor
- Abraham Maslow (1908–1970), professor of psychology
- Will Maslow (1907–2007), lawyer and civil rights leader

Celebrities from Brooklyn

Many celebrities came out of Brooklyn and many of the local high schools like Tilden, Erasmus, Lincoln, and Brooklyn Technical High. These schools produced personalities from every walk of life. This is just one reason why Brooklyn is special.

Here are some celebrities born in Brooklyn: Mickey Rooney, Jackie Gleason, Phil Silvers, Buddy Hackett, Lena Horn, Irwin Shaw, George Gershwin, Barbara Stanwyck, and Spike Lee.

This is the list of some alumni from Thomas Jefferson High:

- Sidney Green, NBA basketball player
- Daniel Keyes, author of *Flowers for Algernon*
- Harry Landers, actor
- Irving Malin, literary critic
- Alan B. Miller, founder, chairman, and CEO of Universal Health Services
- Boris Nachamkin (born 1933), NBA basketball player
- Otis Wilson, linebacker for NFL Chicago Bears
- Shelley Winters, actress
- Jerry Wolkoff, real estate developer
- Max Zaslofsky, NBA basketball player, guard/forward

Growing up in Brooklyn had a great impact on the lives of many talented people like Jerry Seinfeld, Rita Hayworth, and David Blaine.

Some movies that took place in Brooklyn:

The Beast from 20,000 Fathoms
Annie Hall
The Bounty Hunter
Dog Day Afternoon
Godzilla
Goodfellas
Monogamy
The Lords of Brooklyn

Companies founded in Brooklyn:

Topps
Sparrow
Pfizer
P. C. Richard & Sons

Non Graduates from Brooklyn

Danny Kaye was asked to leave the school after a prank involving horse manure and a statue. Entertainers Steve Lawrence and Shelly Winters also attended Jefferson, but I believe they too did not graduate but dropped out to be in show business.

Business people!

Lloyd Blankfein, CEO, Goldman Sachs

The CEO of Goldman Sachs was a 1971 Jefferson grad (and valedictorian.) Born in the Bronx, his family moved to the Linden Houses in the 1950s. He went on to Harvard and a career on Wall Street.

There were many famous people that lived in Brooklyn. Some names you may recognize are Woody Allen, Barbra Streisand, and Joan Rivers. We can't forget Curly and Moe from *The Three Stooges*, who were born in Flatbush. Joey Adams was brought up in Brownsville.

Life goes by Fast

Poem by Martin Blumberg

I'm amazed when I think how fast my life is going
I just wish I was able to slow down the flowing
Just to have me stop and notice
That would have been a tremendous bonus

I would have been able to transmit a picture of each memorable day
That would make my mind clear and not in disarray
In my younger days my brain was vibrant and strong

I knew what was right and also what was wrong
I'll never forget the times I laughed
But also the times I cried
Just recalling those memories brings out my pride

When one is young, they are energetic and able to set the trail
but growing old makes one weak and also frail
But if I had that picture, that would enable me to recall every detail
Where have all the years gone, and why so fast?

I guess there were warnings, but I never once asked
But now since I'm old and gray
I'm grateful to God, each and every day

I feel thankful for the things I have accomplish in life
One that stands out was choosing my wife
And, yes I have regrets about mistakes made in the past

My Brooklyn, My Way

I wish those days can be redone, but they flew by much too fast

Today, I've grown old and lethargic and have lost most of my strength.
But, my mind is still strong to reminisce in length
Hoping my children reflect my thoughts and teach my
grandchildren the same way they were taught
And, the love I have shown them has imbedded in their brain.

I hope they would enjoy life without any pain
Now I have entered the final innings of my life
Knowing there would be more aches and pains
and maybe some strife.

But, I am proud of my journey and I'll do it all again
Hoping my footprint would score a ten
Life is great, and I enjoyed my stay
The reason is, I did it "My way."

Poem

Going Back To Brownsville

by Martin Lewis Blumberg

Now that I've grown old, I hope my wish comes true
A trip back to Brownsville, Brooklyn, a neighborhood where I grew.
I can't wait to visit the stores I once knew.
I wonder if they'll remember me; I just hope they do.
Yes, I'll stop by Amboy Street, where I was born,
I hope I am recognized since my pants are not torn.
I'll take my Spaldeen, just in case we have a game
I hope being old doesn't cause me any pain.
I'll check out the front window, where my mom always sat,
She would probably ask me to put on a sweater or a hat.
I will knock at my door and ask if I could take a peek,
Hoping they would let me in, noticing I was old and weak.
I'll wait on the front stoop until my dad returns from work.
I am sure when he sees me, he'll really have a perk.
But wait, that was over seventy-five years ago, and things may not be the same.
It's possible I won't be remembered, not even my name.
What if my building turned to rubble and the streets are in despair?
Nothing would help me then, not even a prayer.
It may be best to stay away and not go back in time.
As long as I have my memories, that will be sublime.
I could reminisce the experiences of being a boy.
Those were the days that were always such a joy!

My Brooklyn, My Way

by Martin Lewis Blumberg
(sing along to the melody of *My Way*)

And now, the end is near,
And I have reached the final chapter
My friends, I say it clear
So I could share before and after

I wrote my memoir so you can see
My wonderful life, friends and family.
And, yes I have to say
It all took place in "My Brooklyn, My Way"

I never planned a chartered course
And never went past Kings Highway,
Life on Amboy Street was always fun
Especially after Moshe hit that home run

And, yes there were times I'm sure you knew
Annie Hunk ate more cookies then she could chew,
But through it all, when there was doubt
She smelled it twice then spit it out

Regrets I had a few, but not enough to mention
coming home hungry from school finding just dog food
gave me indigestion

These are some of the things I feel you should know

My Brooklyn, My Way

it was like a Broadway show

But all came natural

I've loved, I laughed and cried
But as a child always happy
I slept in a drawer, that's not a fib
I found it more comfortable then sleeping in a crib

And my brother Bob who wrote about the Hunk
And her boyfriend Pacey which he called a punk

And what about Herb who never asked Duvid
How he got to the game
Meeting him 50 years later, then asked him to explain.

Then brother Jack who hit that home run ripping that rookie
Mantle Card as he swung

And last my youngest brother Bruce
Using his sock as a ball
while I deflected his shot
it stuck to the wall

Listening to the Brooklyn Dodgers on the stoop
And smelling the aroma of mom's pea soup

To write the things I truly feel
One may think it's all unreal!
But
Let the records show this is the journey and
memories I want you to know.

Thanks for reading what I have to say,
Hoping my memoirs made your day
Reading My Book
"My Brooklyn, My Way"

My mother's brother Izzy who was killed in WW 11 (1942)

My Mom, Dad with me (1947)

**I am fighting with my brother Jack
because he wants his pants back.
He is telling me that they are too long on
me and he still has another year.**

My mom and her sister Bobbi on the
beach with Jack and me (1946)

Brooklyn basketball team called Lucky 13

My dads mom Annie Blumberg taken
in the late 19th century

My dad's graduation from Junior High

My mother's father Harry Halperin and her brother Bucky

Herb riding his bike on Hopkinson Avenue

Visiting to my brother Herb at his Army base (1951)

A neighbor posing in front of PS175 (1943)

A boy reading the comics on Dumont Avenue

My mom and Herb on Amboy Street (1946)

Picture of my parents and elder brothers

Family posing for a picture on Amboy Street (1946)

171

My friend David's family sitting on the roof on Amboy Street with PS 175 in background

My Dad posing for his Bar Mitzvah (1920)

Jack and me riding a bike (1946)

My friend's sister Roberta taking a stroll down
Amboy Street near Blake Avenue (1948)

The Ambassador Movie Theater

My mom in the early '50s with her new dress

Herb practicing football

My mom holding Bruce and me (1950)

We keep rolling up the cuffs

A Lloyd 60 Party. Still have my business card in case anybody interested

Reunion party (Lloyd 60)

I'm the guy with the rolled up sleeves with muscles

My wife Maxine with our children
with their spouses (2018)

The 5 Blumberg boys celebrating
Bob's 85th Birthday (2015)

My dad with all my brothers at my wedding (1964)

The David Hartman Institute

A Canarsie hangout (1958)

Grand opening specials in Canarsie (1958)

Only seven years old and I couldn't get the girls off my back

Original partners from Auto Barn Stores

Lloyd 60 members going on a date. As you could see Myron got bored, he took a nap

My family's favorite was "Tall in the Saddle"

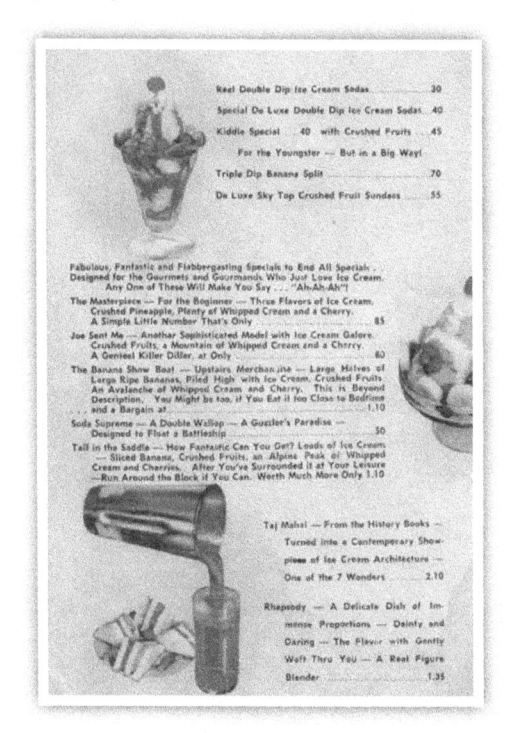

Sol's Menu

179

Epilogue

It's funny the way our minds work. My mind works a little differently from the average person. My short-term memory is terrible. I could see a Broadway show, and the minute I walk outside the theater, I can't remember the name. Ask me where or what I had for dinner, ditto; I have no recall.

But as I have been getting older, my long-term memory seems to be getting better. Different thoughts that I haven't imagined in years seem very memorable. At the age of seventy-eight, I do not want these memories to fade away in vain. I want them to be preserved for future generations. I want my grandchildren and their children to know about my childhood days and how things were in the 1950s.

My three children have heard my stories of Brooklyn since the time they were infants. Before they went to sleep, I would tell them stories. I would first ask them if they wanted me to read them a fairy tale from a book or a true story from when I was a kid; they always picked the latter. I always started out, "When I was a young boy living in Brooklyn." I have shared my stories orally over and over with them, and they always wanted to hear more. It was also told to my grandchildren, and even today, they enjoy listening to my journey through life.

These thoughts and experiences that I have put down on paper are all true. Reminiscing of things that happened in my childhood all came natural. It feels to me that the interaction is happening right at that moment. When I write about my life, family, and friends, I could visualize how they looked, I could look in their faces, and, yes, I could see them smile and I could also see the tears in their eyes.

Now in my later years, right before I fall asleep, I think about those happy years. I think about my mom and dad, I think about my siblings and friends, and I am able to exercise my thoughts without improvising. I could listen and hear what my mom and dad were saying. I laugh at my mom's humor, I hear her singing, and when she is ill, I feel her pain. When I think about my dad, I realize what a hardworking person he was. He was not only street smart, shrewd, but also an intellectual who had a strong knowledge and feelings about many different topics.

I think about my brothers and the close relationships we had growing up in the same household. Even though we played with our own group of friends, there was always a bond that kept us together.

While writing this book about Brooklyn, I realized that the way I am today is a direct reflection of my upbringing. My values, my respect for people, and my love and sympathy for the old or sick are a direct reflection of my past experiences as a young boy.

My memoir of my childhood days that I have written are true. Believe me, these memories couldn't have been made up. My appreciation of my childhood years from Amboy Street to Canarsie should always be remembered and passed on to future generations.

My life was blessed.

As I have noted many times in this book, it was "My Brooklyn, My Way."

—Martin Blumberg

Index

A

Aaron, Larry, 57–58
Amboy Dukes, 18, 109
Amboy Street, 2, 4, 6, 18, 27–28, 55, 62, 74, 76, 88–89, 91, 93, 98, 110, 112, 115, 124
Antonoff, Myron, 128, 152

B

Baseball, 113–14
Baseball cards, 106, 108
Bayview, 121–22, 126, 134, 150
Betsy Head Pool, 42, 123
Blumberg, Frieda, 25
Blumberg, Herb, 11, 14, 30, 32–34, 70–71, 90, 101, 170
Blumberg, Irving, 24–25
Blumberg, Maxine, 34, 133, 140, 142, 151
Blumberg, Robert (Bob), 11, 14–15, 28–32
Borscht Belt, 51–52
Bozzy (uncle), 149
Brill brothers, 98
Brooklyn, 1, 17–18, 55, 65, 74, 88, 116, 121, 126, 131, 150, 158–59
Brooklyn College, 78, 140
Brooklyn Dodgers, 36, 40–41, 47, 106, 113, 117
Brownsville, 1–2, 9, 17, 33, 47, 62, 88, 113, 123, 152, 154–55, 158

C

Canarsie, 42, 123, 126, 134, 140
Cantor, Harvey, 42
Catskill Mountains. *See* Borscht Belt
Charney, Mike, 17, 79, 95
Cherichetti, Lena, 79, 110
Chinatown, 49
Choir, 95–96
Coconut Jim, 18
Coney Island, 65, 111, 123, 129, 131

D

Dembo, Adolph (teacher), xi, 80

E

Ebbets Field, 61
Elowitz, Roger, 153

F

Fortunoff, 74–75, 126
Frazier, Joe, 132, 156

183

G

Goldsmith (doctor), 21
Goldstein, Don "Red," 58
Goldstein, Heshy, 55, 110, 128
Gordon, Sid, 113–14
Grabstein, 149–50
Green (shoemaker), 91–92
Greenberg, Hank, 113
Grosoff (doctor), 21, 29, 32

H

Hartman, David (Duvid), 34
Hebrew School, 97
Heifetz, Molly, 97
Herzl Street, 60, 111
Horn & Hardart, 84
Hymowitz, Roz, 153, 156

J

Joy Garden, 49

K

Kaye, Danny, 161
Kesdin, Murray, 55
Kishke King, 18

L

Lloyd 60, 126, 151–52
Lone Ranger, 100
Lundy's, 67–68

N

Nathan's Famous, 130

P

Pacey (Annie's boyfriend), 29
Peck (teacher), 80
Persky's Mud Garden, 58
Pfizer (choir teacher), 95–96
Pitkin Avenue, 18, 95
Poems
 "Going back to Brooklyn," 164
 "Life goes by to fast," 162
 "Moshe at the Bat," 109
 "My Brooklyn, My Way," 165
 "Post Office Poem," 119
PS 66, *79, 80*
PS 84, *79*
PS 263, *80*

Q

Quonset huts, 42

R

Rappaport (teacher), 81, 139
Robinson, Jackie, 108, 113, 117
Rosen, Al, 113

S

Schultz, Howard, 134
Schwied, Francis, 6–7
Shaw, Gene, 152
Simmons (dentist), 78
Spaldeen, 72, 89, 91, 101, 103, 105, 115
Steeplechase Park, 130
Sukkah, 76

T

Talana (janitor), 62

Thomas Jefferson High School, 80–81, 123, 158
Tilden High School, 27, 33, 58, 70, 80, 122–23
Tonto, 83
Topps, 106, 108, 160

W

Winters, Shelly, 161

CPSIA information can be obtained
at www.ICGtesting.com
Printed in the USA
BVHW071820230321
603272BV00006B/620